YEADON'S REGISTER

of

L N E R

LOCOMOTIVES

Volume Thirty-Three

Class C12, C13, C14, & C17

YEADON'S REGISTER OF L.N.E.R. LOCOMOTIVES - VOLUME 33.

EDITOR'S NOTE & ACKNOWLEDGEMENTS

Getting back to a 'normal' sized volume once again, we keep with the tank engine theme and look at the Atlantic tank engines of Class C12, C13, C14, and the trio of engines inherited from the Midland & Great Northern Railway which constituted LNER Class C17.

For some reason, and we count ourselves amongst that number, many railway enthusiasts and professional railwaymen also, looked upon the Atlantic tank engines as some of the better looking locomotive designs. There was a balance about them which, although it could not be pin pointed, made them look just right whether they be of GN, GC or M&GN design. The equally good looking North British engines of classes C15 and C16 are not covered in this volume and will appear later in the series.

Considering that the 4-4-2 wheel arrangement was not adopted by the LNER for any of its standard designs, the tank engines inherited from the constituents certainly had a longevity about them and the majority worked long enough to become BR property; indeed many lasted until the early years of the 1960's though sadly none were preserved. Perhaps the loss of those engines brought with it a nostalgic affection for something no longer with us.

Once again Eric Fry has done wonders with checking, proof reading and turning over partly hidden stones which have revealed further treasures amongst WBY's wealth of accumulated information.

Mike and Roy continue to bash out the thousands numbers and words which constitute each volume in the series. Thanks gentlemen.

The staff at the Archive of the University of Hull continue to make research an enjoyable experience and thanks go to Heather, Helen and Judy for their continued support and patience.

Jean and Simon Taylor will, we know, enjoy seeing yet another volume of the sries completed but nevertheless it continues with their wholehearted support also. Thanks.

Finally, thanks to you the reader's; your support for the series is much appreciated.

The next *Yeadon's Register of LNER Locomotives*, Volume 34, contains the repair history of the North Eastern and Hull & Barnsley 4-4-0's.

Material contained within this volume has the following catalogue references:
DYE/1/18; DYE/1/19; DYE/1/88; DYE/1/89; DYE/2/2; DYE/2/17; DYE/2/19.

The Yeadon Collection is available for inspection and anyone who wishes to inspect it should contact:-
The Archivist
Brynmor Jones Library
University of Hull
Hull
HU6 7RX
Tel: 01482-465265
A catalogue of the Yeadon collection is available.

First published in the United Kingdom by
BOOK LAW PUBLICATIONS 2004 in association with CHALLENGER
382 Carlton Hill, Nottingham, NG4 1JA.
Printed and bound by The Amadeus Press, Cleckheaton, West Yorkshire.

INTRODUCTION

This volume deals with the one hundred and twelve Atlantic tank engines inherited by the LNER from the Great Central and Great Northern at Grouping. The latter company presented the largest number with sixty locomotives making up LNER Class C12. The Great Central contributed the other fifty-two engines within two classes, LNER C13 and C14. The final three engines, which became LNER Class C17 in July 1942, had arrived in 1936 when the Company swallowed up the Midland & Great Northern Joint Railway. Another fifty-one Atlantic tank engines existed in Scotland but these, encompassed within two classes from the North British Railway (LNER C15 and C16), will be dealt with in a later volume.

C12

Introduced by H.A.Ivatt, Great Northern Railway Class C2 passenger tank engine No.1009 was out-shopped from Doncaster works in February 1898. Nine more, Nos.1010, and 1013 to 1020 followed, somewhat erratically, over the next twelve months and were put to work the lines in the West Riding district where they impressed so much that another fifty were built between 1899 and 1907 for use in the London area. All sixty of the engines were products of Doncaster.

Twenty, Nos.1501 to 1520, entered traffic in 1899 and were similar to the first ten engines except that they and subsequent members of the class had condensing gear. Another ten, Nos.1521 to 1530 were built in 1901 and Nos.1531 to 1540 followed at the end of 1903. The final ten, Nos.1541 to 1550, were constructed in 1907. These handsome 4-4-2 tank engines were then working the bulk of the London suburban passenger services on the GNR. However, even before the last ten appeared, the first of Ivatt's Class N1 0-6-2T's had been constructed and as this class was multiplied they took over the heaviest duties. The building of Gresley's N2 class completed the displacement of the C12's from the London area.

When the LNER came into being most of the former London based C12's had lost their condensing gear and had been dispersed to other areas of the exGN system.

The C12 boiler (LNER Diagram 11) was also standard with other classes such as D4, E1, J4 and J50 (LNER classifications used) and the type was also used occasionally on G1, J7, J55 and J57 classes. Ross 'pop' safety valves replaced the original Ramsbottom type when replacement boilers began to appear during the early years of the LNER period. For further information regarding the Diagram 11 boiler the reader should consult Part 7 of *Locomotives of the LNER*.

Vacuum brakes were standard and between 1901 to 1912 at least a dozen of the class which were working in the West Riding were fitted with vacuum operated brake gear on their bogies. When this gear was discarded from each engine is unknown but it was still in use in 1932.

During the Second World War a plan was drawn up which would enable the services of the Southern Railway and the London Passenger Transport Board to continue in the event of an electrical power disruption caused by enemy action. The plan ensured that over two hundred steam locomotives, presumably all tank engines, were to be made available to work the services on the two systems if certain power stations were bombed or otherwise put out of action. Although it is not absolutely certain,

many of the aforementioned steam locomotives were to be got from the northern companies and ten of the C12's were probably amongst them. The reason for this 'probability' is that ten particular C12's (as recorded in the tables) were called into Doncaster works during the period August to October 1941 for a Light repair. This repair may have entailed reducing the overall width across the cab footsteps, as was done later with J20 and J50 engines for working on SR metals. The ten engines concerned were:- 4511, 4513, 4519, 4523, 4524, 4525, 4528, 4530, 4531 and 4536, all drawn from a diverse selection of sheds such as Bradford, Chester, Hitchin, Louth, etc. At least one C13 tank (6055) was also, unusually, called into Doncaster at this period and might have undergone the same 'repair'.

During August 1921, in order to free its number for the last of Gresley's ten new 3-cylinder 2-6-0 engines (LNER Class K3), No.1009 became 1009A on the Duplicate List. It remained there as No.4009A under the LNER until the 1946 renumbering when it returned to Capital stock as No.7350. Under this renumbering the fifty surviving C12's became 7350 to 7399 in order of their works numbers rather than dates of entry to traffic which, particularly in the case of those built during 1898 and 1901, were out of sequence.

At the start of the BR period five of the class (Nos.7374, 67356, 67363, 67386, 67387) were fitted with push and pull gear which they kept to withdrawal. The gear from 67387 was then put on 67366, in 1955.

As mentioned earlier, this class at first served in the West Riding and London districts but by Grouping had spread their wings somewhat and could be found working local and branch line passenger trains in Nottinghamshire, Cambridgeshire, Lincolnshire, Hertfordshire and Yorkshire. They were equally at home on goods trains and station pilot duties. The West Riding engines worked from Bradford and Ardsley sheds, taking in most of the branches, especially in the hilly district between Halifax and Keighley.

The first moves away from former Great Northern territory happened in the early 1930's when ten of the class moved to Botanic Gardens shed in Hull and started to work the local passenger services radiating from Paragon station to Beverley, Goole and the branches to Hornsea and Withernsea. By 1935 no less than sixteen of the class could be found working in the Hull area.

Also during this time, one engine went to work in the Norwich district of the old Great Eastern. Later a couple more C12's found their way onto the M&GN line at Yarmouth Beach when that line became part of the LNER. Other incursions by the class onto ex GE territory during the next twenty years include working the passenger and goods trains on many of the branch lines in Essex, Norfolk and Suffolk.

During WW2 the class sought pastures anew and found them on the CLC and ex GCR routes around Manchester. Stationed mainly at Trafford Park shed, some fifteen C12's had been based in Lancashire during the years spanning 1940 to 1953. Chester, Gorton and Northwich sheds also had the use of some of those fifteen during the conflict.

On the 27th March 1955, six low mileage C12's were sent from the North Eastern Region (Hull Botanic Gardens shed) to Eastern Region sheds in exchange for six high mileage engines, which were promptly withdrawn. In effect a paper transfer for

The first ten engines were built during 1898 and 1899. Numbered 1009, 1010, and 1013 to 1020, they had square ends to the tanks and bunker, 3ft 3in. chimney and a tall dome cover. Buffers were the parallel shank type with a hollow spindle. Because these ten were for working in the West Riding, they did not have condensing gear fitted but they did have brakes to all bogie wheels. Bradford.

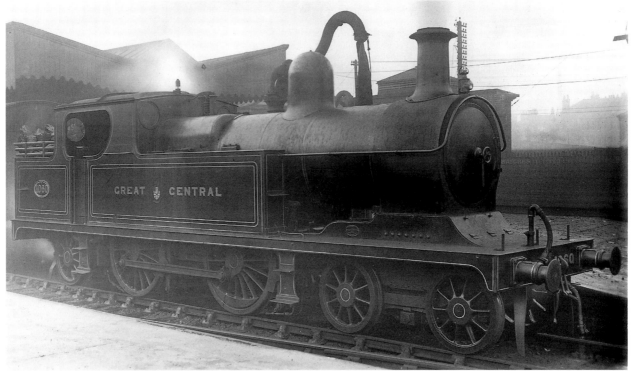

Twelve engines numbered 1055 to 1066 were built between March and June 1903 by Vulcan Foundry. They were all still unsuperheated at Grouping. Note the step on the bunker.

the latter engines. The C12's concerned were:

ER to NER - 67350, 67361, 67375, 67382, 67385, 67389.
NER to ER - 67352, 67391, 67392, 67394, 67395, 67397.

By then, the work of the C12's at Botanic Gardens shed had largely been taken over by former London Midland & Scottish Railway Fowler 2-6-2T's.

Although the first withdrawals took place in April 1937 when four of the class went for scrap, the process of getting rid of the C12's took another twenty-one years. The LNER only managed to cut up eleven and forty-nine became British Railways property although nine of those (7351, 7355, 7358, 7359, 7370, 7377, 7378, 7388 and 7399) never got their BR numbers. The last working C12, No.67397 was condemned in December 1958 and soon scrapped - just a little too early for the preservation movement which later would surely have saved one of these Ivatt engines.

C13

The forty Robinson designed inside cylinder 4-4-2T's, comprising GCR Class 9K, were built in four separate batches between 1903 and 1905. The first twelve, Nos.1055 to 1066, had been delivered by Vulcan Foundry at Newton-le-Willows from March to June 1903. Next, between May and September of the same year and from the GC's own workshops at Gorton came eight engines numbered randomly: 171, 178, 179, 188, 190, 191, 193 and 199. During 1904 another ten engines of the same design appeared from Gorton and these too were just as randomly numbered: 2, 9, 18, 20, 27, 28, 47, 29, 50 and 55 in order of building. The last ten, again untidily and randomly numbered: 457, 454, 455, 456, 310, 57, 59, 114, 115 and 453, came out of Gorton paint shop between January and August 1905.

Ultimately classes C13 and C14 (together with D5 and D6) shared a common design of boiler and it is convenient to deal with both 4-4-2T classes together.

Boilers using saturated steam were fitted when the engines were new. The diameter was 4ft 4in. and barrel and firebox lengths were 10ft 10in. and 6ft 6in. respectively on Class C13, but on C14 there was a slight difference in that the barrel was 2in. longer whilst the firebox was 2in. shorter in length. These differences did not prevent exchanges of boilers between the two classes and from 1912 onwards eight of the C13 boilers found their way onto Class C14 whilst all except one of the C14 boilers saw use on Class C13. One spare boiler had been built in 1908 and five more were made in 1915, with others following. These, and the later superheated variety, had a 6ft 4in. firebox and were known as the No.3 Standard type at Gorton (LNER Diagram No.22).

In 1912 the first ten superheated No.3 boilers were constructed and fitted to the Class D6 4-4-0's, built to Pollitt's design during 1897 to 1899. These had fifteen-element superheaters, but subsequent replacement boilers had eighteen elements. Class C14 No.1122 was superheated in June 1914, the boiler being second-hand and converted from saturated. It was ex C13 No.27 and so had a 10ft 10in. long barrel instead of the by now standard 11ft 0in. This boiler was scrapped in 1923 and No.1122 reverted to saturated state.

Meanwhile a single C13 was superheated. This was No.18 in July 1915 which got a new No.3 standard boiler.

Although superheating of Class D6 continued until wartime conditions caused a temporary halt in 1916, general fitting of

superheated boilers to classes C13 and C14 did not begin until 1926. The task was carried through reasonably quickly and the last C13 to run with a saturated boiler was No.5453, to April 1935. The last C14 had been converted three months earlier. New boilers were used in the main, but some engines were first superheated using second-hand boilers from other C13 and C14 engines whilst eight came from Class D6. Four of those from D6 were from the first batch of replacements built in 1912-13 which had only fifteen superheater elements. These boilers were:

No.110 on	C14	6123	3/35 - 5/37.
No.697 on	C13*	6057	10/32 - 2/35.
No.699 on	C13*	5199	10/30 - 12/32.
		5454	2/33 - 10/35.
		5114	12/35 - 1/38.
No.904 on	C13*	5179	5/29 - 2/32.
	C14*	6122	3/32 - 5/34.
	C13	6055	6/34 - 3/36.

* These were conversions from saturated, the remainder had previously carried boilers with eighteen element superheaters.

Replacement boilers continued to be built, even into BR days, with twenty-two being manufactured during 1948-50. In 1952 three of the old boilers were condemned and in 1953 two more needed scrapping. However, in 1954 five further boilers were condemned and in order to keep the C13 and C14's in traffic, five new boilers Nos.22960 to 22964 were built.

Ramsbottom safety valves were fitted from new and these lasted on the C13's until the 1940's when Ross 'pops' began to appear.

By the end of 1928 the C13's had three separate Class Parts: Part 1 engines comprised the original design built to the GCR gauge; Part 2 covered those engines with the GCR gauge but with superheated boilers; Part 3, which eventually became the class standard, was for engines under 13ft in height and having a superheated boiler. In May 1937 the last engine to become Part 3, No.5453, was converted.

C13's had a steam brake for the engine with vacuum ejector for train working.

Water pick-up gear had been fitted from new to the last twenty engines whilst the first twenty were retro-fitted at Gorton shortly after their building. Because little use was made of the scoops, it was decided to remove the gear from August 1932 and this was accomplished for the whole class by April 1935.

In 1933 six of the class were fitted out for auto-train working. At first mechanical equipment was involved which caused numerous problems not just for fitters but also for drivers and from 1936 vacuum operated gear began to replace the mechanical gear. Two more C13's were fitted out for auto-train working in 1941 but vacuum gear was used from the outset.

As the LNER came into being, those C13's that had gone to the London area from new had mostly migrated northwards from their original home at Neasden and had taken up branch and local passenger duties in the Sheffield area, Manchester and Wrexham. At the latter place the class had been associated with WM&CQ workings from new and remained loyal to that shed for nearly fifty years. Sheffield used the engines on services to Nottingham and Doncaster, besides local services to Barnsley. Trafford Park shed had its engines working on all of its CLC turns. By the mid 1930's half the class were allocated to Gorton shed from where they worked most of the LNER suburban services from Manchester (London Road) station for the next twenty years. Gorton shed also provided the auto-fitted engines for the Oldham, Ashton & Guide Bridge services.

Twelve engines, numbered 1120 to 1131, were built during May and June 1907 by Beyer Peacock & Co., Gorton. Neasden shed.

On 1st October 1936 the LNER took over the engines of the Midland & Great Northern Railway and included amongst them were three 4-4-2-tank engines. Class A on the M&GN, the LNER made them Class C17 but not until July 1942.

Wartime saw three of the class return to the London area in 1941. These were all auto fitted engines for working the Chalfont-Chesham branch, a duty they carried out until 1958 when London Midland Region engines took over.

Under the 1946 renumbering scheme the forty C13's became 7400 to 7439 and all received their BR numbers.

The first withdrawal came in December 1952 (67435) but it was to be January 1960 before this class was finally extinct with the condemnation of No.67417 at Gorton.

C14

These twelve engines, Nos.1120 to 1131, which were delivered by Beyer, Peacock in 1907, were a modified design of the C13's with greatly increased coal and water capacity making them nearly 4$\frac{1}{2}$ tons heavier. Classified 9L on the GCR, they shared the same saturated boiler. For further details regarding these boilers and superheating, etc., the reader is referred to Class C13 above.

Steam brake for engine and vacuum ejector for train working followed the same pattern as the C13 class.

Regarding the three Class Parts used for the C14's, these mirrored the C13 engines in virtually every respect and likewise had disappeared by June 1937.

This class was also fitted with water pick-up gear similar to the C13's. It too became redundant by the 1930's and was removed virtually over the same time period.

All the C14's went new to Neasden shed for working the Marylebone suburban services. However, larger motive power in the shape of the new 4-6-2T (LNER Class A5) from 1911 onwards meant that the C14's, along with the C13's, were no longer needed in London and they began to leave in 1912. At first the C14 class worked from various sheds on the main line, their endurance being useful for working stopping trains. At Grouping the majority of the class were allocated to Annesley shed and thereafter they spent periods at Colwick and Langwith Junction.

In 1927 No.6126 went to Hitchin for a three year stint including a short stay at Hatfield. Its duties at Hitchin included working Baldock trains and standing in for the railcar on the Hertford line. No.6126 returned north to Colwick but was off south again in 1935 to former Great Eastern country where, accompanied by six other C14's, they made a home of Ipswich shed, where they were particularly associated with the Felixstowe branch workings. An eighth member of the class, No.6120, had arrived in East Anglia during the previous year and in 1938 they were joined by No.6130. During the war the class worked from other exGER sheds, Cambridge, King's Lynn, Lowestoft and Norwich all having their services during 1940 and 1941 after which the C14's began to drift away from the area some returning to Neasden, others to Manchester whilst new ground was again broken with the arrival of three engines at Ardsley. However, the C14 association with East Anglia lasted until 1950 when the last three, all still allocated to Ipswich shed, were sent away ousted by more powerful motive power in the shape of Thompson's L1 tanks.

In the early BR years new sheds for this class included Lincoln and Wrexham and in 1950 Bradford where the exiles from Ipswich ended up. In 1955 all the class, except two at Wrexham, were working the Manchester suburban trains from Gorton shed and most remained on those duties until the end. Three went to Barnsley in 1957 after being made redundant in Manchester by the newly introduced diesel railcars.

During 1946 they were renumbered 7440 to 7451 and all received BR numbers.

Withdrawals of the C14's started somewhat later than the C13 class, in January 1957 (67451) and by January 1960 the C14 had also been wiped out with the condemnation of No.67450.

C17

The Midland & Great Northern Railway Class A tank engine class comprised three locomotives, all of which were built at Melton Constable in different years of the twentieth century - No.41 in 1904; No.20 in 1909 and No.9 in 1910. They were taken over by the LNER from 1st October 1936 but were not classified C17 by the LNER until July 1942.

The outline design was based somewhat on the M&GN's Beyer, Peacock supplied 4-4-0's and the London, Tilbury & Southend 4-4-2T's though many of the parts making up each engine had originated from standard Derby and Doncaster drawings. Steam brake for the engine and vacuum ejector for train working was normal for all three throughout their lives.

The 6ft 0in. driving wheels were ideal for handling the passenger services on the none too fast lines of the M&GNR and it was this kind of work to which the trio kept to all their lives. During their M&GN days, the class was split up seasonally and were shedded variously at Cromer, Melton Constable, South Lynn and Yarmouth Beach. The LNER also tended to keep the engines working within the boundaries of the former Eastern Section of the M&GN allocating them to Melton Constable for the most part.

The LNER simply added a zero as a prefix to the original numbers and although two engines lasted long enough to have new numbers allotted in the 1943 renumbering scheme, neither of them received those allotted numbers 7503 (041), and 7504 (09), before they were condemned in 1944. All three were painted in unlined black during the LNER period, in line with policy at that time. All repairs were carried out at Stratford and all three were scrapped there too.

Being latecomers to the LNER fold, and especially being a class only three strong, the C17's LNER operational life expectancy could only be regarded as short. However, when they were finally withdrawn after only six to eight years service to the LNER it must be remembered that they were already over thirty years old (041 was nearly forty years old), which was approximately the expected average life span for a steam locomotive.

The first engine of the next batch, No.1501 built February 1899, was similar except that it had rounded corners to its tanks and bunker, and the buffers were taper shank with beaded ends and solid spindles. Initially it carried condensing gear but this was removed in December 1900 when it was transferred from Hatfield to the West Riding. Copley Hill shed.

The other nineteen built in 1899, Nos. 1502 to 1520 were for the London area, so had 2ft 5in. chimney, medium height dome, no bogie brakes but they did have destination board brackets fitted on the smokebox door and the rear of the bunker (*see* page 10, top). All had condensing apparatus with a straight brass pipe from the top of the smokebox, except on No.1520 which had a cast iron pipe from the base of the smokebox. Nos.1521 to 1530 were built in 1901, also for the London area and these had the straight pipe type of condensing gear. King's Cross shed.

CLASS C 12

4009A

Doncaster 755.

To traffic 2/1898.

REPAIRS:
Don. ?/?—?/5/14.**G.**
Don. 16/1—28/4/23.**G.**
Don. 4/1—17/426.**G.**
Don. 31/1—14/3/29.**G.**
Don. 27/7—27/8/31.**G.**
Don. 7/12/33—8/1/34.**G.**
Don. 24/7—15/8/36.**G.**
Don. 17/6—22/7/39.**G.**
Don. 22/8—5/9/42.**G.**
Don. 19/1—16/2/46.**G.**
Don. 17—23/7/47.**L.**
Don. 16/9—29/10/48.**G.**
Don. 23/1—20/2/52.**G.**
Don. 13/4/55. *Not repaired.*

BOILERS:
1009.
1511 5/14.
1172 28/4/23.
8165 14/3/29.
8316 15/8/36.
7820 22/7/39.
21855 20/2/52.

SHEDS:
Bradford.
Northwich 30/3/40.
Chester 6/1/41.
Northwich 29/11/42.
Melton Constable 26/2/43.
Trafford Park 10/8/43.
Langwith Jct. 12/2/45.
Lincoln 5/8/45.
Boston 31/7/49.
New England 28/6/53.
Botanic Gardens 27/3/55.

RENUMBERED:
4009A 17/4/26.
7350 22/12/46.
67350 29/10/48.

CONDEMNED: 13/4/55.
Cut up at Doncaster.

4010

Doncaster 756.

To traffic 2/1898.

REPAIRS:
Don. ?/?—?/8/19.**G.**

Don. 8/1—31/3/23.**G.**
Don. 2/2—25/4/25.**G.**
Don. 21/7—28/10/27.**G.**
Don. 8/2—8/3/30.**G.**
Don. 19/3—9/4/32.**G.**
Don. 12/10—2/11/35.**G.**
Don. 18—25/12/37.**G.**
Don. 8—22/3/41.**G.**
Don. 18/10—8/11/41.**L.**
Don. 6/5—3/6/44.**G.**
Don. 30/3—12/5/47.**G.**
Don. 9/11/48. *Not repaired.*

BOILERS:
1010.
1463 8/19.
7820 28/10/27.
8169 25/12/37.

SHEDS:
Copley Hill.
Chester 19/7/43.
Trafford Park 29/8/43.
Langwith Jct. 20/5/45.

RENUMBERED:
4010 25/4/25.
7351 22/9/46

CONDEMNED: 1/12/48.
Cut up at Doncaster.

4013

Doncaster 757.

To traffic 5/1898.

REPAIRS:
Don. ?/?—?/8/18.**G.**
Don. 23/8—12/11/21.**G.**
Don. 18/6—13/10/23.**G.**
Don. 10/12/24—28/3/25.**G.**
Don. 18/12/25—6/3/26.**H.**
Don. 12/3—9/8/28.**G.**
Don. 29/11—27/12/30.**G.**
Don. 11/2—11/3/33.**G.**
Don. 10/8—7/9/35.**G.**
Don. 31/12/38—21/1/39.**G.**
Don. 8/2—1/3/41.**G.**
Don. 16—23/8/41.**L.**
Don. 27/3—17/4/43.**G.**
Don. 22/7—5/8/44.**G.**
Don. 22/12/45—19/1/46.**H.**
Don. 4—27/2/48.**G.**
Don. 22—28/7/48.**L.**
Don. 6—20/10/48.**L.**
Don. 19/4—21/5/51.**G.**
Don. 15—23/4/52.**C/L.**
Don. 1—20/5/53.**C/L.**

Don. 3/6—9/7/54.**G.**
Don. 19/11/58. *Not repaired.*

BOILERS:
1013.
1016 8/18.
8148 27/12/30.
9508 19/1/46.
21822 21/5/51.
21911 9/7/54.

SHEDS:
Bradford.
Copley Hill 7/6/37.
Louth 14/6/37.
Botanic Gardens 12/7/53.
New England 27/3/55.
Spital Bridge 20/11/55.
Grantham 7/7/57.

RENUMBERED:
1013N 13/10/23.
4013 28/3/25.
7352 29/9/46.
E7352 27/2/48.
67352 28/7/48.

CONDEMNED: 19/11/58.
Cut up at Doncaster.

4014

Doncaster 758.

To traffic 3/1898.

REPAIRS:
Don. ?/?—?/8/11.**G.**
Don. 10/11/21—11/2/22.**G.**
Don. 12/3—16/8/24.**G.**
Don. 20/12/26—12/3/27.**G.**
Don. 22/6—20/7/29.**G.**
Don. 31/12/31—23/1/32.**G.**
Don. 8—29/12/34.**G.**
Don. 15/8—5/9/36.**G.**
Don. 16/12/39—20/1/40.**G.**
Don. 8—29/5/43.**G.**
Don. 14/4—5/5/45.**L.**
Don. 21/9—12/10/46.**G.**
Don. 4—30/3/51.**G.**
Don. 6/4/55. *Not repaired.*

BOILERS:
1014.
1510 8/11.
1475 11/2/22.
8516 23/1/32.
8481 12/10/46.
21819 30/3/51.

SHEDS:
Copley Hill.
Ardsley 15/4/51.
Copley Hill 23/12/51.
Ardsley 2/11/52.
Copley Hill 14/6/53.
Botanic Gardens 12/7/53.

RENUMBERED:
4014 16/8/24.
7353 10/11/46.
67353 30/3/51.

CONDEMNED: 12/4/55.
Cut up at Doncaster.

4015

Doncaster 788.

To traffic 10/1898.

REPAIRS:
Don. ?/?—?/12/11.**G.**
Don. ?/?—?/3/19.**G.**
Don. 12/12/21—18/2/22.**G.**
Don. 15/5—28/7/23.**G.**
Don. 1/2—28/4/26.**G.**
Don. 7/3—26/5/28.**G.**
Don. 25/10—15/11/30.**G.**
Don. 16—30/11/35.**G.**
Don. 15—29/5/37.**L.**
Tablet exch. app fitted.
Don. 14/10—11/11/39.**G.**
Don. 27/3—17/4/43.**G.**
Don. 17—31/3/45.**G.**
Don. 12/11/47—11/1/48.**G.**
Don. 13/7—1/8/48.**L.**
Don. 1—18/8/50.**C/L.**
Don. 17/4—11/5/51.**G.**
Don. 17/12/51-4/1/52.**C/L.**
Don. 24—29/1/53.**C/L.**
Don. 26/5/53. *Not repaired.*

BOILERS:
1015.
1463 12/11.
1452 3/19.
6988 26/5/28.
8445 15/11/30.
7925 31/3/45.
21821 11/5/51.

SHEDS:
Bradford.
Louth *by* 1924.
Yarmouth Beach 25/5/37.
Melton Constable 19/5/42.
Norwich 9/4/47.
Melton Constable 1/6/47.

4015 cont./
Cambridge 1/8/48.
Melton Constable 10/10/48.
Cambridge 12/12/48.
Botanic Gardens 30/1/50.

RENUMBERED:
4015 28/4/26.
7354 15/12/46.
67354 31/7/48.

CONDEMNED: 22/6/53.
Cut up at Doncaster.

4016

Doncaster 789.

To traffic 10/1898.

REPAIRS:
Don. ?/?—?/8/16.**G.**
Don. 30/1—12/5/23.**G.**
Don. 26/4—25/9/26.**G.**
Don. 12/1—13/2/29.**G.**
Don. 4/7—1/8/31.**G.**
Don. 8—22/2/36.**G.**
Don. 31/10—7/11/36.**L.**
Don. 1—15/10/38.**G.**
Don. 27/12/41—24/1/42.**G.**
Don. 9/6—21/7/45.**G.**

BOILERS:
1016.
6817 8/16.
8170 13/2/29.
8685 22/2/36.
8147 15/10/38.

SHEDS:
Lincoln
Norwich 14/3/33.
Lowestoft 13/5/33.
Ipswich 24/8/33.
Parkeston 7/4/34.
Cambridge 12/10/38.
Colwick 29/11/38.
Trafford Park 16/10/41.
Langwith Jct. 12/2/45.
Louth 24/11/46.
Langwith Jct. 26/1/47.

RENUMBERED:
4016 25/9/26.
7355 1/12/46.

CONDEMNED: 5/3/48.
Cut up at Doncaster.

4017

Doncaster 790.

To traffic 10/1898.

REPAIRS:
Don. ?/?—?/6/14.**G.**
Don. 18/11/19—7/2/20.**G.**
Don. 11/6—25/8/23.**G.**
Don. 7—29/11/24.**L.**
Don. 12/3—24/7/26.**G.**
Don. 26/9—24/11/27.**G.**
Don. 14/11/28—3/1/29.**G.**
Don. 21/2—14/3/31.**G.**
Don. 17/3—7/4/34.**G.**

BOILERS:
1017.
1283 6/14.
 399 24/7/26.
8169 3/1/29.

SHED:
Bradford.

RENUMBERED:
4017 29/11/24.

CONDEMNED: 24/4/37.
Cut up at Doncaster.

4018

Doncaster 791.

To traffic 12/1898.

REPAIRS:
Don. ?/?—?/12/14.**G.**
Don. 18/3—1/7/22.**G.**
Don. 25/9—10/12/25.**G.**
Don. 12/6—21/9/28.**G.**
Don. 9/5—6/6/31.**G.**
Don. 21/10—18/11/33.**G.**
Don. 25/1—15/2/36.**G.**
Don. 13—27/8/38.**G.**
Don. 28/11—19/12/42.**G.**
Don. 14/7—11/8/45.**G.**
Don. 14/12/48—12/1/49.**G.**
Don. 23/4—5/5/49.**C/L.**
Push & pull fitted.
Don. 6/9/51. *Not repaired.*

BOILERS:
1018.
1514 12/14.
6915 10/12/25.
8143 21/9/28.
8508 15/2/36.

8549 11/8/45.
8677 12/1/49.

SHEDS:
Bradford.
Copley Hill 9/6/46.
King's Cross 8/5/49.
South Lynn 24/6/51.
King's Lynn 8/7/51.

RENUMBERED:
4018 10/12/25.
7356 9/12/46.
67356 12/1/49.

CONDEMNED: 1/10/51.
Cut up at Doncaster.

4019

Doncaster 796.

To traffic 10/1898.

REPAIRS:
Don. ?/?—?/3/13.**G.**
Don. 16/9—6/11/20.**G.**
Don. 23/4—20/8/23.**G.**
Don. 17/2—29/5/26.**G.**
Don. 17/8—21/9/29.**G.**
Don. 22/2—14/3/36.**G.**
Don. 13/5—15/7/39.**G.**
Don. 13/9—11/10/41.**G.**
Don. 22/7—5/8/44.**G.**
Don. 6/2—8/3/47.**G.**
Don. 16/1—7/2/51.**G.**
Don. 15/2—10/3/54.**G.**
Don. 22/5/58. *Not repaired.*

BOILERS:
1019.
1014 3/13.
7033 20/8/23.
8303 21/9/29.
8170 14/3/36.
9253 11/10/41.
21902 *(new)* 7/2/51.
21909 10/3/54.

SHEDS:
Ardsley
Louth 11/6/26.
New Holland 14/7/30.
Botanic Gardens 14/8/34.
Louth 16/6/37.
Langwith Jct. 1/6/42.
New England 27/2/49.

RENUMBERED:
4019 29/5/26.

7357 6/10/46.
67357 7/2/51.

CONDEMNED: 22/5/58.
Cut up at Doncaster.

4020

Doncaster 797.

To traffic 2/1899.

REPAIRS:
Don. ?/?—?/12/12.**G.**
Don. 23/8—26/11/21.**G.**
Ard. 29/8—5/9/23.**L.**
Don. 23/3—14/8/25.**G.**
Don. 23/11/25—6/2/26.**L.**
Don. 23/10—30/11/28.**G.**
Don. 24/10—14/11/31.**G.**
Don. 30/12/33—27/1/34.**G.**
Don. 18/4—9/5/36.**G.**
Don. 25/2—15/4/39.**G.**
Don. 23/8—20/9/41.**G.**
Don. 23/9—14/10/44.**G.**

BOILERS:
1020.
1015 12/12.
6835 26/11/21.
 793 14/8/25.
8168 30/11/28.
8766 9/5/36.
9251 20/9/41.

SHEDS:
Bradford.
Copley Hill 4/4/35.
Trafford Park 7/5/46.

RENUMBERED:
4020 14/8/25.
7358 8/9/46.

CONDEMNED: 16/1/48.
Cut up at Doncaster.

4501

Doncaster 812.

To traffic 2/1899.

REPAIRS:
Don. ?/?—?/5/09.**G.**
Don. 17/7—2/12/22.**G.**
Don. 21/7—24/10/25.**G.**
Don. 17/11/27—15/3/28.**G.**
Don. 22/2—22/3/30.**G.**

WORKS CODES:- Cw - Cowlairs. Dar- Darlington. Don - Doncaster. Ghd - Gateshead. Gor - Gorton. Inv - Inverurie. Nor - Norwich. Str - Stratford.
REPAIR CODES:- **C/H** - Casual Heavy. **C/L** - Casual Light. **G** - General. **H**- Heavy. **H/I** - Heavy Intermediate. **L** - Light. **L/I** - Light Intermediate. **N/C** - Non-Classified.

8

The remaining twenty, Nos.1531 to 1550 built 1903 to 1907 and for London area, were fitted with condensing apparatus from the base of the smokebox. Like No.1520, Nos.1531 to 1550 had parallel shank buffers instead of the taper shank type fitted to the earlier engines.

By Grouping the forty-nine condenser-fitted engines had lost their workings to the 1921-built N2 tanks and the condensing apparatus had been removed from most of them. On some of the straight pipe type, the smokebox outlet was simply blanked off. Note the step on the bunker and the handgrip near to the cab roof.

Removal of the condensing apparatus took place from 1921 onwards as they went to Doncaster for repair and by Grouping only sixteen remained to be dealt with. The task was completed in December 1924 except for two engines.

Only two, Nos.4541 and 4550, still had their condensing apparatus when they got LNER livery (*see also* page 20, top). It was removed from No.4550 when ex works on 8th December 1927 but No.4541 had gone out on 30th September 1927 still fitted. When next in works, on 1st February 1930, it was recorded that the apparatus had been removed, so this must have been done at a shed. Note extra brackets for London area lamp codes.

(above) The original boilers had Ramsbottom safety valves in a cast iron cover.

All the replacement boilers built after Grouping had Ross 'pop' safety valves, usually fitted directly onto the firebox.

(above) **From August 1918 to May 1927, No.4522 carried an 1899 built boiler on which Ross 'pops' had been fitted onto the Ramsbottom mounting.**

(right) **In October 1927, No.4522 was ex works with a 1927 built boiler with the 'pops' mounted directly onto the firebox. Note the change of chimney from 2ft 5in. to 3ft 3in. type.**

There were also cases of the shorter chimney being combined with the tall dome cover, and this was also a 1927 built boiler. Copley Hill shed.

Some went straight from the London area shorter chimney and dome to both of the full height. No.1537 received these ex works on 26th May 1923 and it remained at Hatfield shed until January 1927.

Beginning in 1940, a 2ft 10in. high chimney was introduced to bring some within the 13ft 0in. gauge so that they could traverse the Sheffield-Manchester line and work in the Manchester area. Note two top lamp irons fitted.

4501 cont./
Don. 17/6—15/7/33.**G**.
Don. 16/5—6/6/36.**G**.
Don. 5—26/11/38.**G**.
Don. 6/12/41—3/1/42.**G**.
Don. 10/6—8/7/44.**G**.
Don. 2—9/6/45.**L**.
Don. 27/10—10/11/45.**L**.
Don. 23/3—6/4/46.**L**.
Don. 26/1—1/3/47.**G**.
Don. 28/3—14/4/47.**L**.

BOILERS:
1501.
1502 5/09.
1467 24/10/25.
8062 15/3/28.
8769 6/6/36.

SHEDS:
Copley Hill.
Northwich 30/3/40.
Chester 6/1/41.
Trafford Park 4/11/41.
Langwith Jct. 16/7/42.
Louth 11/8/42.

RENUMBERED:
4501 24/10/25.
7359 13/4/46.

CONDEMNED: 22/8/49.
Into Don. for cut up 25/8/49.

4502

Doncaster 813.

To traffic 3/1899.

REPAIRS:
Don. ?/?—?/2/08.**G**.
Don. ?/?—?/12/12.**G**.
Don. 5/4—16/7/21.**G**.
Don. 1/5—8/8/25.**G**.
Don. 4/10—10/11/28.**G**.
Don. 18/3—22/4/33.**G**.
Don. 13—27/2/37.**H**.
Tablet exch. app. fitted.
Don. 18/11—16/12/39.**G**.
Don. 1—23/7/44.**G**.
Tablet exch. app. removed.
Don. 19/5—7/6/47.**L**.
Don. 11/3—6/5/48.**G**.
Don. 8/5—7/6/51.**G**.

BOILERS:
1502.
1509 2/08.
1465 12/12.
8161 10/11/28.
8165 23/7/44.
21823 7/6/51.

SHEDS:
Hatfield *at* 10/1/23.
Boston *by* 9/23.
Yarmouth Beach 2/3/37.
Norwich 17/2/40.
Cambridge 26/5/40.
Melton Constable 22/7/40.
Norwich 14/12/40.
Cambridge 28/12/40.
Bury St Edmunds 19/10/52.
Cambridge 19/7/53.
King's Lynn 4/10/53.

RENUMBERED:
4502 8/8/25.
7360 7/4/46.
67360 6/5/48.

CONDEMNED: 22/1/55.
Into Don. for cut up 24/1/55.

4503

Doncaster 814.

To traffic 3/1899.

REPAIRS:
Don. ?/?—?/12/07.**G**.
Don. ?/?—?/1/14.**G**.
Don. 29/9/21—7/1/22.**G**.
Don. 23/7—8/11/24.**G**.
Don. 19/9—1/12/27.**G**.
Don. 22/2—22/3/30.**G**.
Don. 14/4—5/5/34.**G**.
Don. 5/8—2/9/39.**G**.
Don. 16/10—6/11/43.**G**.
Don. 26/10—22/11/46.**G**.
Don. 5/12/49—13/1/50.**G**.
Don. 29/10—1/12/52.**G**.
Don. 15/4/55. *Not repaired.*

BOILERS:
1503.
1511 12/07.
1523 1/14.
7823 1/12/27.
8151 2/9/39.
8302 22/11/46.
8679 13/1/50.
21884 1/12/52.

SHEDS:
Louth
Hornsey 5/5/34.
Peterborough East 17/5/37.
New England 30/4/39.
Botanic Gardens 27/3/55.

RENUMBERED:
4503 8/11/24.
7361 16/6/46.
67361 13/1/50.

CONDEMNED: 15/4/55.
Cut up at Doncaster.

4504

Doncaster 815.

To traffic 3/1899.

REPAIRS:
Don. ?/?—?/2/08.**G**.
Don. ?/?—?/6/18.**G**.
Don. 28/5—31/7/20.**G**.
Don. 28/5—20/9/24.**G**.
Don. 20/6—7/10/27.**G**.
Don. 10/10—7/11/31.**G**.
Don. 20/6—11/7/36.**G**.
Don. 6—27/1/40.**G**.
Don. 27/11—18/12/43.**G**.
Don. 14/1—1/2/47.**G**.
Don. 17/7—11/8/50.**G**.
Don. 3/9—8/10/53.**G**.
Don. 11/1/58. *Not repaired.*

BOILERS:
1504.
1513 2/08.
1529 6/18.
8517 7/11/31.
10572 11/8/50.
21944 8/10/53.

SHEDS:
Boston.
New England 26/9/34.
Spital Bridge 20/8/50.
Grantham 16/5/54.

RENUMBERED:
4504 20/9/24.
7362 12/5/46.
67362 11/8/50.

CONDEMNED: 11/1/58.
Cut up at Doncaster.

4505

Doncaster 816.

To traffic 4/1899.

REPAIRS:
Don. ?/?—?/4/06.**G**.
Don. 26/1—27/3/20.**G**.
Don. 8/10—20/12/24.**G**.
Don. 26/5—13/8/27.**G**.
Don. 11/4—2/5/31.**G**.
Don. 15/12/34—5/1/35.**G**.
Don. 31/12/38—21/1/39.**G**.
Don. 19/12/42—9/1/43.**G**.
Don. 2—23/3/46.**H**.

Don. 26/1—18/2/49.**G**.
Push & pull gear fitted.
Don. 9—31/1/51.**G**.
Don. 1/7—5/8/54.**G**.
Don. 13/11—22/12/56.**G**.
Don. 20/11/58. *Not repaired.*

BOILERS:
1505.
1623 4/06.
6989 27/3/20.
7951 2/5/31.
8484 5/1/35.
8761 18/2/49.
21901 *(new)* 31/1/51.
21822 5/8/54.
21880 22/12/56.

SHEDS:
New England.
Annesley 20/2/49.
Stratford 31/5/53.
Annesley 23/8/53.
Tilbury 14/10/56.
New England 24/8/58.

RENUMBERED:
4505 20/12/24.
7363 30/5/46.
67363 18/2/49.

CONDEMNED: 20/11/58.
Cut up at Doncaster.

4506

Doncaster 817.

To traffic 4/1899.

REPAIRS:
Don. ?/?—?/11/06.**G**.
Don. ?/?—?/9/16.**G**.
Don. 22/7—22/10/21.**G**.
Don. 25/8—21/11/25.**G**.
Don. 18/2—5/6/26.**H**.
New cylinders.
Don. 18/5—22/6/29.**G**.
Don. 8/9—6/10/34.**G**.
Don. 18/9—2/10/37.**G**.
Don. 3—24/5/41.**G**.
Don. 5—26/8/44.**G**.
Don. 21/4—5/5/45.**L**.
Don. 25/5—2/8/47.**G**.
Don. 22/8—3/9/48.**L**.
Don. 10/11—10/12/48.**H**.
Don. 13/8—18/9/50.**G**.
Don. 14/10—18/11/53.**G**.
Don. 25/5/56. *Not repaired.*

BOILERS:
1506.
1505 11/06.

13

4506 cont./
1099 9/16.
6964 21/11/25.
8675 6/10/34.
8548 2/10/37.
8318 2/8/47.
8770 10/12/48.
21800 18/9/50.
21904 18/11/53.

SHEDS:
Louth
New England 14/7/30.
Colwick 25/6/35.
Trafford Park 16/10/41.
Langwith Jct. 16/7/42.
Lincoln 8/7/45.
Louth 20/11/45.
Lincoln 5/5/46.
Louth 11/1/48.

RENUMBERED:
4506 21/11/25.
7364 21/7/46.
67364 3/9/48.

CONDEMNED: 25/5/56.
Cut up at Doncaster.

4507

Doncaster 818.

To traffic 4/1899.

REPAIRS:
Don. ?/?—?/8/09.**G.**
Don. ?/?—?/7/14.**G.**
Don. 11/4—4/10/22.**G.**
Don. 3/10—26/12/25.**G.**
Don. 2/3—13/4/29.**G.**
Don. 13/8—3/9/32.**G.**
Don. 17—24/9/32.**L.**
Don. 16/11—7/12/35.**G.**
Don. 14/8/37.**L.**
Don. 6/4—4/5/40.**G.**
Don. 13—27/11/43.**G.**
Don. 30/4—3/6/47.**G.**
Don. 24/5—23/6/50.**G.**
Don. 9/7—5/8/53.**G.**
Don. 22/5/58. *Not repaired.*

BOILERS:
1507.
1514 8/09.
1009 7/14.
1466 26/12/25.
8159 13/4/29.
8482 3/6/47.
8769 23/6/50.
21913 5/8/53.

SHED:
New England

RENUMBERED:
4507 26/12/25.
7365 29/9/46.
67365 23/6/50.

CONDEMNED: 22/5/58.
Cut up at Doncaster.

4508

Doncaster 819.

To traffic 5/1899.

REPAIRS:
Don. ?/?—?/12/06.**G.**
Don. ?/?—?/5/15.**G.**
Don. 7/1—15/4/22.**G.**
Don. 21/9—28/11/25.**G.**
Don. 27/7—24/8/29.**G.**
Don. 26/8—7/10/33.**G.**
Don. 12—31/12/36.**G.**
Don. 13/12/41—10/1/42.**G.**
Don. 30/9—21/10/44.**G.**
Don. 4/3—2/4/48.**G.**
Don. 18/3—21/4/50.**G.**
Gor. 22/5—2/6/51.**C/L.**
Don. 25/2—11/3/52.**G.**
Gor. 16/12/52—17/1/53.**C/L.**
Don. 10/6—15/7/54.**G.**
Don. 31/3—14/4/55.**N/C.**
Push & pull fitted.
Don. 12—24/8/55.**C/L.**
Don. 25/4—14/5/57.**C/L.**
Don. 3/4/58. *Not repaired.*

BOILERS:
1508.
6817 12/06.
1506 5/15.
6816 15/4/22.
7816 7/10/33.
8509 31/12/36.
8142 21/10/44.
8159 21/4/50.
21865 15/7/54.

SHEDS:
New England.
Boston 15/1/37.
Northwich 21/2/40.
Langwith Jct. 12/7/42.
Trafford Park 6/5/46.
Chester 14/5/46.
Trafford Park 11/4/48.
New England 8/2/53.
Spital Bridge 15/2/53.
New England 2/1/55.
Yarmouth 13/4/55.

RENUMBERED:
4508 28/11/25.
7366 6/10/46.
67366 2/4/48.

CONDEMNED: 3/4/58.
Cut up at Doncaster.

4509

Doncaster 820.

To traffic 5/1899.

REPAIRS:
Don. ?/?—?/10/07.**G.**
Don. ?/?—?/11/14.**G.**
Don. 5/12/19—21/2/20.**G.**
Don. 23/10/23—2/2/24.**G.**
Don. 6/8—18/12/26.**G.**
Don. 30/11—21/12/29.**G.**
Don. 13/2—5/3/32.**G.**
Don. 5/5—2/6/34.**G.**
Don. 1—22/8/36.**G.**
Don. 11/5—1/6/40.**G.**
Don. 4—25/9/43.**G.**
Don. 3—31/8/46.**G.**
Don. 22/1—14/2/51.**G.**
Don. 26/10—18/11/54.**G.**
Don. 20/6—5/7/55.**C/L.**
Don. 25/4—9/5/56.**C/L.**
Don. 9—26/10/56.**C/L.**
Don. 6/8/58. *Not repaired.*

BOILERS:
1509.
1506 10/07.
1017 11/14.
1127 18/12/26.
8317 21/12/29.
8168 22/8/36.
8162 31/8/46.
21903 *(new)* 14/2/51.
21900 18/11/54.

SHEDS:
Boston.
New England *by* 1924.
Cambridge 1/3/38.
Ipswich 11/8/49.
Cambridge 13/10/49.
Bury St Edmunds 19/10/52.
Cambridge 19/7/53.
King's Lynn 1/11/53.
Cambridge 20/11/55.
Bury St Edmunds ?
Spital Bridge 24/3/57.
Grantham 7/7/57.

RENUMBERED:
1509N 2/2/24.
4509 18/12/26.
7367 26/5/46.
67367 14/2/51.

CONDEMNED: 6/8/58.
Cut up at Doncaster.

4510

Doncaster 821.

To traffic 5/1899.

REPAIRS:
Don. ?/?—?/9/10.**G.**
Don. 3/5—17/9/21.**G.**
Don. 4/8—24/10/25.**G.**
Don. 14/12/29—11/1/30.**G.**
Don. 4—25/3/33.**G.**
Don. 7/9—12/10/35.**G.**
Don. 19/2—12/3/38.**G.**
Don. 19/10—16/11/40.**G.**
Don. 30/10—20/11/43.**G.**
Don. 9/6—28/7/47.**G.**
Don. 14/1—28/2/50.**G.**
Don. 19/12/52—24/1/53.**G.**
Don. 25/10—11/11/54.**C/L.**
Don. 24/10/55. *Not repaired.*

BOILERS:
1510.
1504 9/10.
8319 11/1/30.
8163 12/3/38.
8326 28/2/50.
21887 24/1/53.

SHEDS:
Boston.
New England *by* 1930.
Boston 2/12/35.
New England 29/1/36.
Spital Bridge 12/4/53.

RENUMBERED:
4510 24/10/25.
7368 13/10/46.
67368 28/2/50.

CONDEMNED: 26/10/55.
Cut up at Doncaster.

4511

Doncaster 832.

To traffic 8/1899.

REPAIRS:
Don. ?/?—?/3/07.**G.**
Don. 21/10/20—5/3/21.**G.**
Don. 19/3—16/8/24.**G.**
Don. 18/1—27/2/26.**G.**
Don. 1/4—23/9/27.**G.**
Don. 28/9—19/10/29.**G.**
Don. 24/9—29/10/32.**G.**
Don. 31/8—28/9/35.**G.**
Don. 18/3—15/4/39.**G.**
Don. 9—16/8/41.**L.**
Modification of footsteps.
Don. 20/11—11/12/43.**G.**

(above) **This medium length chimney, combined with a tall dome cover, was still in use on British Railways. This is a 25th July 1953 working at Beccles and the photo of 7350 on page 42, bottom, shows another on 13th September 1958.**

(right) **The original boiler handrail arrangement was of the continuous variety and some kept this type to withdrawal. Note that a doorstop has been fitted. Doncaster works.**

Some were changed to have the handrail terminating on the side of the smokebox, with a short cross rail fitted on the door. This change was not directly concerned with the fitting of a doorstop.

At least two, 4009ᴀ by May 1946 and 67384 by December 1948 had both a continuous rail and one on the door.

The destination board brackets remained long after the C12 class left the London area and after the Nottingham District ceased to use them. From before Grouping to 1949, No.4505 was at New England shed and destination boards were never used around Peterborough.

4511 cont./
Don. 23/11/47—16/1/48.**G.**
Don. 19/4—19/5/50.**G.**
Gor. 30/11—8/12/51.**C/L.**
Don. 8/7/54. *Not repaired.*

BOILERS:
1511.
1427 3/07.
6836 5/3/21.
7816 23/9/27.
8554 29/10/32.
9817 16/1/48.
8142 19/5/50.

SHEDS:
Colwick.
Hitchin 10/11/32.
Chester 16/7/43.
Trafford Park 5/9/43.
New England 8/2/53.

RENUMBERED:
4511 16/8/24.
7369 10/10/46
ᴇ7369 16/1/48
67369 29/1/49

CONDEMNED: 19/7/54.
Cut up at Doncaster.

_____

4512

Doncaster 833.

To traffic 8/1899.

REPAIRS:
Don. ?/?—?/2/11.**G.**
Don. ?/?—?/5/16.**G.**
Don. 14/4—6/8/21.**G.**
Don. 30/10/24—31/1/25.**G.**
Don. 25/8—12/11/27.**G.**
Don. 3—24/10/31.**G.**
Don. 2—16/2/35.**G.**

BOILERS:
1512.
1521 2/11.
1474 5/16.
7821 12/11/27.
7382 16/2/35.

SHEDS:
Hatfield *at* 10/1/23.
Grantham ????.
Lincoln *by* 12/23.
New England 19/11/27.
Peterborough East 19/9/34.
New England 29/12/34.

RENUMBERED:
4512 31/1/25.

CONDEMNED: 10/4/37.
Cut up at Doncaster.

_____

4513

Doncaster 834.

To traffic 8/1899.

REPAIRS:
Don. ?/?—?/9/07.**G.**
Don. ?/?—?/8/16.**G.**
Don. 7/10—4/12/20.**G.**
Don. 11/8—1/11/24.**G.**
Don. 26/4—29/7/27.**G.**
Don. 2/11—7/12/29.**G.**
Don. 24/11—8/12/34.**G.**
Don. 3—17/10/36.**G.**
Don. 20/8—3/9/38.**G.**
Don. 14/6—5/7/41.**G.**
Don. 16/8/41.**L.**
Modification of footsteps.
Don. 19/9—3/10/42.**H/I.**
Don. 11/8—8/9/45.**G.**
Don. 4/1/48. *Not repaired.*

BOILERS:
1513.
1508 9/07.
1521 8/16.
8315 7/12/29.
8317 17/10/36.
7924 3/9/38.
8675 5/7/41.
8164 3/10/42.

SHEDS:
Louth.
New Holland. 14/7/30.
Louth 17/5/34.
New Holland. 1/1/35.
Colwick 25/6/35.
Annesley 28/1/40.
Trafford Park 28/7/43.

RENUMBERED:
4513 1/11/24.
7370 5/10/46.

CONDEMNED: 30/1/48.
Cut up at Doncaster.

_____

4514

Doncaster 835.

To traffic 9/1899.

REPAIRS:
Don. ?/?—?/3/09.**G.**
Don. ?/?—?/11/13.**G.**
Don. 14/4—23/7/21.**G.**
Don. 24/8—14/11/25.**G.**

Don. 6/2—20/4/28.**G.**
Don. 16/8—20/9/30.**G.**
Don. 10/12/32—7/1/33.**G.**
Don. 6—27/4/35.**G.**
Don. 17/7—7/8/37.**G.**
Don. 26/8—7/10/39.**G.**
Don. 4—25/4/42.**G.**
Don. 22/1—5/2/44.**G.**
Don. 11/5—15/6/46.**H.**
Don. 20/9—16/10/48.**G.**
Don. 7/2—2/3/51.**G.**
Don. 27/11—7/12/51.**C/L.**
Don. 7/4—1/5/53.**G.**
Don. 10—18/2/54.**C/L.**
Don. 21—30/9/54.**N/C.**
Don. 29/3/55. *Not repaired.*

BOILERS:
1514.
1522 3/09.
1509 11/13.
8068 20/4/28.
8515 27/4/35.
8765 *(ex 4545)* 7/10/39.
8685 *(ex 4531)* 15/6/46.
21905 *(new)* 2/3/51.
21892 1/5/53.

SHEDS:
Hatfield *at* 10/1/23.
Lincoln *by* 12/23.
Botanic Gardens 30/9/30.

RENUMBERED:
4514 14/11/25.
7371 12/10/46.
67371 15/10/48.

CONDEMNED: 4/4/55.
Cut up at Doncaster.

_____

4515

Doncaster 836.

To traffic 10/1899.

REPAIRS:
Don. 18/11/20—9/4/21.**G.**
Don. 15/9—20/12/24.**G.**
Don. 18/3—28/5/27.**G.**
Don. 24/8—28/9/29.**G.**
Don. 29/6—13/7/35.**G.**

BOILERS:
1515.
1603 9/4/21.
8305 28/9/29.

SHEDS:
Colwick.
Langwith Jct. 21/6/30.
Colwick 11/3/31.
Langwith Jct. 25/3/31.

Colwick 1/11/34.

RENUMBERED:
4515 20/12/24.

CONDEMNED: 24/6/37.
Cut up at Doncaster.

_____

4516

Doncaster 837.

To traffic 10/1899.

REPAIRS:
Don. ?/?—?/11/16.**G.**
Don. 14/12/21—25/2/22.**G.**
Don. 5/10—19/12/25.**G.**
Don. 15/2—27/4/28.**G.**
Don. 21/2—14/3/31.**G.**
Don. 17/8—28/9/35.**G.**

BOILERS:
1516.
1519 11/16.
345 25/2/22.
8065 27/4/28.

SHEDS:
New England.
Lincoln 30/3/31.
Colwick 11/2/36.

RENUMBERED:
4516 19/12/25.

CONDEMNED: 27/11/37.
Cut up at Doncaster.

_____

4517

Doncaster 838.

To traffic 10/1899.

REPAIRS:
Don. 20/5—3/7/20.**G.**
Don. 22/8—1/12/23.**G.**
Don. 16/7—5/11/26.**G.**
Don. 3—31/8/29.**G.**
Don. 26/11—24/12/32.**G.**
Don. 15—29/6/35.**L.**
Don. 7—21/11/36.**G.**
Don. 15—22/10/38.**G.**
Don. 19/6—17/7/43.**G.**
Don. 1—15/1/44.**G.**
Don. 19/8—2/9/44.**L.**
Don. 5/1—15/2/47.**G.**
Don. 27/11—22/12/50.**G.**

BOILERS:
1517.
6842 3/7/20.

8301 31/8/29.
8688 21/11/36.
8675 15/1/44.
21811 22/12/50.

SHEDS:
Colwick.
Botanic Gardens 25/7/34.
Bradford 26/10/37.
Northwich 22/3/40.
Trafford Park 8/8/42.
Copley Hill 23/2/47.

RENUMBERED:
1517N 1/12/23.
4517 5/11/26.
7372 13/4/46.
67372 22/12/50.

CONDEMNED: 18/5/53.
Cut up at Doncaster.

4518

Doncaster 839.

To traffic 10/1899.

REPAIRS:
Don. ?/?—?/5/14.**G.**
Don. 16/9—26/11/21.**G.**
Don. 17/8—24/10/25.**G.**
Don. 16/2—3/5/28.**G.**
Don. 13/2—5/3/32.**G.**
Don. 25/5—22/6/35.**G.**
Don. 5—12/11/38.**G.**
Don. 16/5—6/6/42.**G.**
Don. 1—22/9/45.**G.**
Don. 1—30/11/48.**G.**
Don. 21/2/51. *Not repaired.*

BOILERS:
1518.
1288 5/14.
1122 26/11/21.
8069 3/5/28.
8508 22/9/45.
8309 30/11/48.

SHEDS:
Boston.
New England 20/12/32.

RENUMBERED:
4518 24/10/25.
7373 2/6/46.
67373 27/11/48.

CONDEMNED: 5/3/51.
Cut up at Doncaster.

4519

Doncaster 840.

To traffic 11/1899.

REPAIRS:
Don. ?/?—?/9/16.**G.**
Don. 9/11/20—19/3/21.**G.**
Don. 5/2—5/5/23.**G.**
Don. 23/11/25—13/2/26.**G.**
Don. 24/10—7/12/28.**G.**
Don. 18/10—15/11/30.**G.**
Don. 3—24/3/34.**G.**
Don. 20/2—6/3/37.**G.**
Don. 14/10—11/11/39.**G.**
Don. 9—16/8/41.**L.**
Modification of footsteps.
Don. 6/12/41—3/1/42.**G.**
Don. 27/11—18/12/43.**G.**
Don. 20/10—17/11/45.**G.**
Don. 21/11—31/12/47.**G.**
Don. 3/1/48.**N/C.**
Push & pull fitted.
Don. 9/1—2/2/51.**G.**
Don. 21/9—15/10/54.**G.**
Don. 20—25/10/54.**N/C.**
Don. 2/4/58. *Not repaired.*

BOILERS:
1519.
1116 9/16.
6994 5/5/23.
8171 7/12/28.
8488 24/3/34.
7950 31/12/47.
21900 *(new)* 2/2/51.
21841 15/10/54.

SHEDS:
Colwick.
Annesley 14/3/28.
Colwick 22/10/28.
Botanic Gardens 16/7/34.
Louth 16/6/37.
King's Cross 2/1/48.
South Lynn 24/6/51.
King's Lynn 8/7/51.

RENUMBERED:
4519 13/2/26.
7374 20/10/46.
67374 2/2/51.

CONDEMNED: 2/4/58.
Cut up at Doncaster.

4520

Doncaster 841.

To traffic 11/1899.

REPAIRS:
Don. ?/?—?/7/16.**G.**
Don. 22/2—7/5/21.**G.**
Don. 19/2—24/5/24.**G.**
Don. 14/9—25/12/26.**G.**
Don. 17/8—7/9/29.**G.**
Don. 23/7—13/8/32.**G.**
Don. 11/4—2/5/36.**G.**
Don. 18/6—2/7/38.**G.**
Don. 1—22/3/41.**G.**
Don. 9—23/12/44.**G.**
Don. 21/6—23/7/48.**G.**
Don. 1/12/50—1/1/51.**G.**
Don. 27/2—14/4/54.**C/L.**
Don. 20—22/4/54.**N/C.**
Don. 5/4/55. *Not repaired.*

BOILERS:
1520.
1527 7/16.
7032 24/5/24.
8302 7/9/29.
8767 2/5/36.
8065 2/7/38.
8557 23/7/48.
21813 1/1/51.

SHEDS:
Colwick.
Botanic Gardens 16/7/34.
Ardsley 7/11/38.
Cambridge 27/12/38.
March 23/3/52.
Bury St Edmunds 19/10/52.
Botanic Gardens 27/3/55.

RENUMBERED:
4520 24/5/24.
7375 24/9/46.
67375 23/7/48.

CONDEMNED: 5/4/55.
Cut up at Doncaster.

4521

Doncaster 924.

To traffic 6/1901.

REPAIRS:
Don. ?/?—?/11/10.**G.**
Don. ?/?—?/2/16.**G.**
Don. 15/3—14/6/19.**G.**
Don. 18/4—1/9/23.**G.**
Don. 9/7—11/12/26.**G.**
Don. 9/8—20/9/30.**G.**
Don. 28/4—26/5/34.**G.**

Don. 16—23/4/38.**G.**
Don. 13/6—16/7/42.**G.**
Don. 12/1—2/2/46.**G.**
Don. 9—23/6/50.**C/H.**
Don. 21/7—17/8/53.**G.**
Don. 22/5/58. *Not repaired.*

BOILERS:
1521.
1464 11/10.
1480 2/16.
7824 20/9/30.
8155 23/4/38.
7924 16/7/42.
10570 23/6/50.
21898 17/8/53.

SHEDS:
New England.
Hornsey 5/5/46.
New England 14/1/51.

RENUMBERED:
4521 30/3/25.
7376 2/11/46.
67376 23/6/50.

CONDEMNED: 22/5/58.
Cut up at Doncaster.

4522

Doncaster 925.

To traffic 6/1901.

REPAIRS:
Don. ?/?—?/10/08.**G.**
Don. ?/?—?/8/18.**G.**
Don. 3/3—14/5/21.**G.**
Don. 3/6—6/9/24.**G.**
Don. 27/5—27/10/27.**G.**
Don. 29/8—10/10/31.**G.**
Don. 4—25/8/34.**G.**

BOILERS:
1522.
1503 10/08.
1505 8/18.
7817 27/10/27.

SHEDS:
New England.
Peterborough East 29/12/34.

RENUMBERED:
4522 6/9/24.

CONDEMNED: 1/6/37.
Cut up at Doncaster.

WORKS CODES:- Cw - Cowlairs. Dar- Darlington. Don - Doncaster. Ghd - Gateshead. Gor - Gorton. Inv - Inverurie. Nor - Norwich. Str - Stratford.
REPAIR CODES:- C/H - Casual Heavy. C/L - Casual Light. G - General. H- Heavy. H/I - Heavy Intermediate. L - Light. L/I - Light Intermediate. N/C - Non-Classified.

This redundant fitting on No.4505 was duly recognised and they were taken off, probably at the May 1931 repair.

Surprisingly, the destination board brackets could still be seen to October 1948 on No.7380 (ex 4527) which spent all the LNER years at Grantham.

Engines which had condensing apparatus had a feed pump for supplying the boiler and a clack box on each side.

Non-condensing engines had boilers supplied through injectors on the faceplate.

(below) All acquired injectors on the faceplate but by 1930 these were being superseded by flood type fitted behind the cab footsteps.

The first ten had a perfectly straight sided bunker surmounted by two open coal rails and these remained unaltered at least until 1927. Note that the step on the bunker and the handgrip on the cab had still not been added. These ten had a vertical handrail on the front of the side tanks.

A bunker top flared out at the sides and back but still surmounted by two open coal rails was introduced with No.1530 when built and Nos.1502 to 1529 were soon altered to correspond. Nos.1501 to 1550, which had rounded front corners to the side tanks, did not have the vertical handrail on the tank ends. Instead, a hand grip was fitted to the frames near the leading footsteps. Although a Nottingham engine by Grouping, No.4519 still had London lamp irons at least to 1928.

On the first engine so fitted, No.1530, the flared sides of the bunker top projected further forward than on any of the others.

(above) This bunker top feature on No.4530 only, remained through the LNER years and to withdrawal as BR No.67383.

(left) No.7359 was previously No.4501 and thus the first built with the rounded corners to the tanks and bunker. being allocated to the West Riding, when coal rails were added these were of the type fitted to the first ten engines, the flared section being omitted.

4523

Doncaster 926.

To traffic 6/1901.

REPAIRS:
Don. ?/?—?/9/13.**G.**
Don. 1/5—23/9/22.**G.**
Don. 8/12/24—14/3/25.**G.**
Don. 11/7—5/9/28.**G.**
Don. 4/7—8/8/31.**G.**
Don. 23/6—21/7/34.**G.**
Don. 10—24/10/36.**G.**
Don. 24/12/38—4/2/39.**G.**
Don. 27/9—4/10/41.**L.**
Modification of footsteps.
Don. 11—25/7/42.**G.**
Don. 2—23/3/46.**G.**
Don. 18/7/49. *Not repaired.*

BOILERS:
1523.
1473 9/13.
1440 23/9/22.
8509 8/8/31.
8165 24/10/36.
8155 25/7/42.
8265 23/3/46.

SHEDS:
Colwick.
Annesley 7/27.
Colwick 14/3/28.
Northwich 2/12/39.
Gorton 25/7/42.
Trafford Park 6/11/42.
Doncaster 25/3/45.
Copley Hill 2/8/45.
Boston 20/6/48.

RENUMBERED:
4523 14/3/25.
7377 22/9/46.

CONDEMNED: 18/7/49.
Cut up at Doncaster.

4524

Doncaster 927.

To traffic 10/1901.

REPAIRS:
Don. ?/?—?/12/15.**G.**
Don. 7/10/20—26/2/21.**G.**
Don. 15/9—20/12/24.**G.**
Don. 14/9—19/11/27.**G.**
Don. 1/2—1/3/30.**G.**
Don. 17/12/32—28/1/33.**G.**
Don. 22/2—14/3/36.**G.**
Don. 26/3—2/4/38.**G.**
Don. 7—24/9/38.**L.**

Don. 23/12/39—23/3/40.**L.**
Don. 9—16/8/41.**L.**
Modification to footsteps.
Don. 19/9—3/10/42.**G.**
Don. 2/6—7/7/45.**G.**

BOILERS:
1524.
1018 12/15.
1450 20/12/24.
7822 19/11/27.
8155 28/1/33.
7819 2/4/38.

SHEDS:
Colwick.
Annesley 15/2/27.
Colwick ?/7/27.
Botanic Gardens 20/7/34.
Bradford 5/11/37.
Ardsley 9/12/37.
Bradford 7/6/42.
Trafford Park 5/5/46.

RENUMBERED:
4524 20/12/24.
7378 10/11/46

CONDEMNED: 16/1/48.
Cut up at Doncaster.

4525

Doncaster 928.

To traffic 8/1901.

REPAIRS:
Don. ?/?—?/4/16.**G.**
Don. 18/3—24/6/22.**G.**
Don. 3/10/23—12/1/24.**G.**
Don. 7/12/25—6/3/26.**G.**
Don. 13/3—5/10/28.**G.**
Don. 11/7—1/8/31.**G.**
Don. 30/7—27/8/32.**G.**
Don. 25/1—8/2/36.**G.**
Don. 25/3—29/4/39.**G.**
Don. 18/1—8/2/41.**G.**
Don. 30/8—6/9/41.**L.**
Modification of footsteps.
Don. 25/9—16/10/43.**G.**
Don. 24/3—21/4/45.**G.**
Don. 20/10/45.**L.**
Don. 18/12/46—11/1/47.**G.**
Don. 5/10—4/11/49.**G.**
Don. 25/7—24/8/51.**G.**
Don. 26/4—25/5/54.**G.**
Don. 19/10/54.*Weigh.*
Don. 10/6/58. *Not repaired.*

BOILERS:
1525.
1464 4/16.
8147 5/10/28.

8679 8/2/36.
8265 4/11/49.
21836 24/8/51.
21907 25/5/54.

SHEDS:
Grantham.
Louth 14/2/25.
Spital Bridge 23/10/55.
New England 20/11/55.

RENUMBERED:
1525N 12/1/24.
4525 6/3/26.
7379 29/9/46.
67379 4/11/49.

CONDEMNED: 10/6/58.
Cut up at Doncaster.

4526

Doncaster 929.

To traffic 9/1901.

REPAIRS:
Don. ?/?—?/11/18.**G.**
Don. 10/1—7/2/20.**G.**
Don. 9/10/23—5/1/24.**G.**
Don. 1/7—27/10/26.**G.**
Don. 9/2—23/3/29.**G.**
Don. 26/9—17/10/31.**G.**
Don. 29/9—13/10/34.**G.**

BOILERS:
1526.
6843 11/18.
8163 23/3/29.

SHED:
Colwick.

RENUMBERED:
1526N 5/1/24.
4526 24/3/25.

CONDEMNED: 10/4/37.
Cut up at Doncaster.

4527

Doncaster 930.

To traffic 6/1901.

REPAIRS:
Don. ?/?—?/3/16.**G.**
Don. 2/11/21—11/3/22.**G.**
Don. 27/8—22/11/24.**G.**
Don. 4/12/26—26/3/27.**G.**
Don. 21/9—19/10/29.**G.**
Don. 18/2—4/3/33.**G.**

Don. 28/3—18/4/36.**G.**
Don. 18/11—9/12/39.**G.**
Don. 10/4—1/5/43.**G.**
Don. 25/5—22/6/46.**G.**
Don. 12—29/10/48.**G.**
Don. 5/9—8/10/51.**G.**
Don. 13/4—14/5/54.**G.**
Don. 30/5/58. *Not repaired.*

BOILERS:
1527.
6840 3/16.
1514 26/3/27.
8309 19/10/29.
8488 29/10/48.
21844 8/10/51.
21902 14/5/54.

SHEDS:
Grantham.
Spital Bridge 6/6/54.
New England 28/10/56.

RENUMBERED:
4527 22/11/24.
7380 24/3/46.
67380 29/10/48.

CONDEMNED: 30/5/58.
Cut up at Doncaster.

4528

Doncaster 931.

To traffic 11/1901.

REPAIRS:
Don. ?/?—?/3/19.**G.**
Don. 12/1—27/5/22.**G.**
Don. 29/6—3/10/25.**G.**
Don. 31/12—13/2/26.**L.**
Don. 5/7—24/8/28.**G.**
Don. 7—28/2/31.**G.**
Don. 25/11—30/12/33.**G.**
Don. 4—25/7/36.**G.**
Don. 25/3—22/4/39.**G.**
Don. 30/11—21/12/40.**L.**
Don. 16—23/8/41.**L.**
Modification of footsteps.
Don. 25/7—1/8/42.**G.**
Don. 16/2—9/3/46.**G.**
Don. 31/12/48—27/1/49.**G.**
Don. 13/12/51. *Not repaired.*

BOILERS:
1528.
1515 3/19.
6835 3/10/25.
8151 30/12/33.
8062 25/7/36.
8317 22/4/39.

4528 cont./
SHEDS:
Ardsley.
Grantham 14/2/25.
Ardsley 27/2/31.
Bradford 6/3/31.
Chester 30/3/40.
Gorton 7/5/42.
Trafford Park 14/3/43.
Doncaster 11/3/45.
Barnsley 29/7/45.
Lincoln 28/10/45.
Louth 20/10/46.
Lincoln 19/1/47.
Louth 4/9/49.

RENUMBERED:
4528 3/10/25.
7381 9/10/46
67381 27/1/49

CONDEMNED: 21/1/52.
Cut up at Doncaster.

___

4529

Doncaster 932.

To traffic 10/1901.

REPAIRS:
Don. ?/?—?/7/16.**G.**
Don. 12/9—10/12/21.**G.**
Don. 4/7—11/10/24.**G.**
Don. 1/11—19/2/27.**G.**
Don. 29/6—3/8/29.**G.**
Don. 30/7—27/8/32.**G.**
Don. 10/4—1/5/37.**G.**
Don. 28/12/40—18/1/41.**G.**
Don. 12/12/42—9/1/43.**L.**
After collision.
Don. 17/6—15/7/44.**G.**
Don. 4/2—15/3/47.**G.**
Don. 9/11—2/12/49.**G.**
Don. 2—31/7/52.**G.**
Don. 6/4/55. *Not repaired.*

BOILERS:
1529.
1524 7/16.
6993 11/10/24.
8067 27/8/32.
7818 1/5/37.
8550 2/12/49.
8550 Re-no. 21875 31/7/52.

SHEDS:
Grantham.
Botanic Gardens 27/3/55.

RENUMBERED:
4529 11/10/24.
7382 22/9/46.
67382 2/12/49.

CONDEMNED: 6/4/55.
Cut up at Doncaster.

___

4530

Doncaster 933.

To traffic 11/1901.

REPAIRS:
Don. ?/?—?/5/17.**G.**
Don. 12/12/19—28/2/20.**G.**
KX. 30/9—14/10/20.**L.**
Don. 10/10/23—19/1/24.**G.**
Don. 30/6—23/10/26.**G.**
Don. 19/1—23/2/29.**G.**
Don. 11/7—8/8/31.**G.**
Don. 22/2—14/3/36.**G.**
Don. 29/10—12/11/38.**G.**
Don. 23/8—6/9/41.**L.**
Modification of footsteps.
Don. 20/2—20/3/43.**G.**
Don. 7—21/10/44.**G.**
Don. 30/3—27/4/46.**G.**
Don. 27/11—30/12/49.**G.**
Don. 28/7—23/8/52.**G.**
Don. 3/5/54.Weigh.
Don. 31/1/55. *Not repaired.*

BOILERS:
1530.
6989 5/17.
1606 28/2/20.
8164 23/2/29.
8686 14/3/36.
7818 30/12/49.
21916 *(new)* 23/8/52.

SHEDS:
Colwick.
Langwith Jct. 17/10/29.
Colwick 4/1/30.
Bradford 27/6/33.
Copley Hill 9/6/46.
Boston 20/6/48.
Lincoln 27/2/49.
Louth 27/8/50.

RENUMBERED:
1530ₙ 19/1/24.
4530 23/10/26.
7383 8/9/46.
67383 30/12/49.

CONDEMNED: 31/1/55.
Cut up at Doncaster.

___

4531

Doncaster 1017.

To traffic 12/1903.

REPAIRS:
Don. ?/?—?/2/13.**G.**

REPAIRS:
Don. ?/?—?/1/11.**G.**
Don. 31/10/19—14/2/20.**G.**
Don. 6/1—14/4/23.**G.**
Don. 15/6—4/9/25.**G.**
Don. 27/9—25/12/26.**G.**
Don. 22/12/27—22/2/28.**G.**
Don. 30/10—14/11/28.**L.**
Don. 28/12/28—11/1/29.**L.**
Don. 3/5—7/6/30.**G.**
Don. 10—31/1/31.**G.**
Don. 11/11—2/12/33.**G.**
Don. 4—18/7/36.**G.**
Don. 18/11—9/12/39.**G.**
Don. 21—23/8/41.**L.**
Modification of footsteps.
Don. 13/12/41.**L.**
Don. 29/5—26/6/43.**G.**
Don. 22—29/4/44.**L.**
Don. 5/1—9/2/46.**G.**
Don. 4—25/5/47.**G.**
Don. 28/11—28/12/48.**G.**
Don. 13/3—4/4/52.**G.**
Don. 16/9—15/10/54.**G.**
Don. 19—22/10/54.**N/C.**
Don. 4/5/56. *Not repaired.*

BOILERS:
1463.
1472 1/11.
7038 4/9/25.
8326 7/6/30.
8164 18/7/36.
8685 9/12/39.
8677 9/2/46.
8314 28/12/48.
21860 4/4/52.
21851 15/10/54.

SHEDS:
Copley Hill.
Ardsley 7/12/37.
Chester 30/3/40.
Trafford Park 7/12/41.
Gorton 8/3/42.
Langwith Jct. 23/6/43.
Louth 28/8/49.

RENUMBERED:
4531 4/9/25.
7384 6/10/46.
67384 28/12/48.

CONDEMNED: 7/5/56.
Cut up at Doncaster.

___

4532

Doncaster 1018.

To traffic 12/1903.

REPAIRS:
Don. ?/?—?/2/13.**G.**

Don. 25/12/20—23/4/21.**G.**
Don. 18/8—29/11/24.**G.**
Don. 8/6—6/10/27.**G.**
Don. 28/9—26/10/29.**G.**
Don. 9/4—14/5/32.**G.**
Don. 9/9—14/10/33.**G.**
Don. 17/8—21/9/35.**G.**

BOILERS:
1473.
1020 2/13.
7818 6/10/27.
8157 21/9/35.

SHED:
Copley Hill 16/8/13.

RENUMBERED:
4532 29/11/24.

CONDEMNED: 29/4/37.
Cut up at Doncaster.

___

4533

Doncaster 1019.

To traffic 12/1903.

REPAIRS:
Don. ?/?—?/6/10.**G.**
Don. ?/?—?/11/15.**G.**
Don. 23/1—20/5/22.**G.**
Don. 8/12/24—14/3/25.**G.**
Don. 8/6—16/11/27.**G.**
Don. 20/6—26/7/30.**G.**
Don. 19/11—10/12/32.**G.**

BOILERS:
1474.
1477 6/10.
6837 11/15.
7819 16/11/27.

SHEDS:
Grantham 14/12/21.
New England *after* 1/1/23.
Immingham 19/11/27.
Lincoln *by* 1/1/35.
Louth 23/7/35.
Lincoln 8/10/35.
New Holland 28/4/37.

RENUMBERED:
4533 14/3/25.

CONDEMNED: 10/12/37.
Cut up at Doncaster.

___

In 1908, No.1509 had the bunker back plate curved upwards at the centre, and grids turned inward to conform so as to keep coal clear of the rear windows, which were changed from circular to triangular. The bunker arrangement soon reverted to normal but the triangular rear windows remained on No.4509 to withdrawal as No.67367 in August 1958.

By 1911 all had been fitted with steam heating connection at both ends and these were retained.

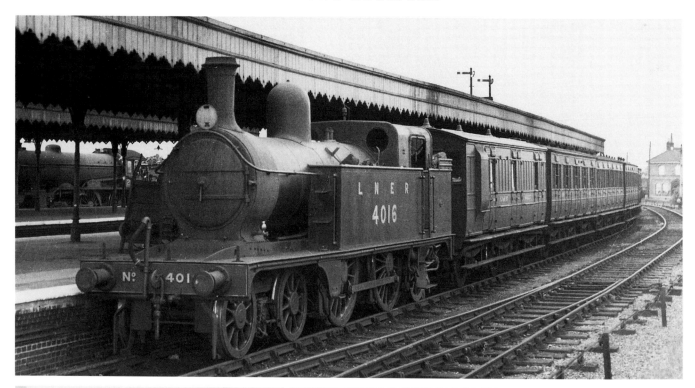

(above) The vacuum brake on the engine also operated blocks on the bogie wheels of the first ten Nos.1009, 1010, and 1013 to 1020, and they were added to No.1501 *(see* page 6, top) when it became a West Riding engine. They were also put on No.1514 in January 1907.

(left) The Leeds Copley Hill engines Nos.4010, 4014, 4020 and 4501 still had the bogie brakes at November 1936 but they were cut out and inoperative due to difficulty in keeping them workable. All C12's so fitted had the bogies brakes removed after 1939.

So that they could be used on the Midland & Great Northern line, two of the class were fitted with Whittaker type tablet exchanging apparatus, No.4502 in March 1937. Note this engine also changed from taper to parallel shank buffers.

4534

Doncaster 1020.

To traffic 12/1903.

REPAIRS:
Don. ?/?—?/10/14.**G.**
Don. 22/3—22/7/22.**G.**
Don. 26/1—18/4/25.**G.**
Don. 21/2—14/5/27.**G.**
Don. 30/11—21/12/29.**G.**
Don. 28/7—18/8/34.**G.**
Don. 16—23/3/35.**L.**
Don. 15—29/2/36.**G.**
Don. 2—9/7/38.**G.**
Don. 30/1—27/2/43.**G.**
Don. 13/12/46—22/1/47.**G.**
Don. 9/12/50—9/1/51.**G.**
Don. 1/4/55. *Not repaired.*

BOILERS:
1480.
1518 10/14.
6841 14/5/27.
8316 21/12/29.
8147 29/2/36.
7824 9/7/38.
21815 9/1/51.

SHEDS:
Hatfield *at* 10/1/23.
Colwick ?/?
Langwith Jct. 15/7/27.
Botanic Gardens 27/8/34.
Bradford 11/11/37.
Cambridge 5/8/38.
Ipswich 6/8/49.
Cambridge 13/10/49.
March 27/7/52.
Bury St Edmunds. 19/10/52.
Botanic Gardens 27/3/55.

RENUMBERED:
4534 18/4/25.
7385 3/11/46.
67385 9/1/51.

CONDEMNED: 1/4/55.
Cut up at Doncaster.

4535

Doncaster 1021.

To traffic 12/1903.

REPAIRS:
Don. ?/?—?/4/14.**G.**
Don. 28/5—21/8/20.**G.**
Don. 6/11/23—19/1/24.**G.**
Don. 14/9—18/12/26.**G.**
Don. 2/2—23/3/29.**G.**
Don. 18/7—8/8/31.**G.**

Don. 13/1—10/2/34.**G.**
Don. 25/7—8/8/36.**G.**
Don. 7/1/39. *Not repaired.*

BOILERS:
1469.
1522 4/14.
1134 19/1/24.
8166 23/3/29.
8144 8/8/36.

SHED:
Copley Hill.

RENUMBERED:
1535N 19/1/24.
4535 18/12/26.

CONDEMNED: 21/1/39.
Cut up at Doncaster.

4536

Doncaster 1022.

To traffic 12/1903.

REPAIRS:
Don. ?/?—?/8/10.**G.**
Don. ?/?—?/2/16.**G.**
Don. 21/10/20—26/2/21.**G.**
Don. 7/7—25/10/24.**G.**
Don. 13/5—29/7/27.**G.**
Don. 27/7—24/8/29.**G.**
Don. 16/1—20/2/32.**G.**
Don. 10/11—1/12/34.**G.**
Don. 20/2—6/3/37.**G.**
Don. 27/4—25/5/40.**G.**
Don. 27/9—11/10/41.**L.**
Modification of footsteps.
Don. 24/7—21/8/43.**G.**
Don. 5/5—21/7/45.**G.**
Don. 30/8—24/9/48.**G.**
Don. 14/2—2/3/49.**C/L.**
Push & pull fitted.
Don. 31/3—11/4/49.**C/L.**
Don. 31/7—29/8/51.**G.**
Don. 23/11—23/12/54.**G.**
Don. 29—31/12/54.**N/C.**
Don. 3/4/58. *Not repaired.*

BOILERS:
1472.
1474 8/10.
1477 2/16.
8549 20/2/32.
8445 21/7/45.
8554 24/9/48.
21837 29/8/51.
21811 23/12/54.

SHEDS:
Bradford.
Ardsley 22/12/37.

Copley Hill 20/6/43.
Ardsley 3/3/49.
King's Lynn 16/9/51.
Stratford 26/9/54.
King's Lynn 14/11/54.

RENUMBERED:
4536 25/10/24.
7386 19/5/46.
67386 24/9/48.

CONDEMNED: 3/4/58.
Cut up at Doncaster.

4537

Doncaster 1023.

To traffic 12/1903.

REPAIRS:
Don. ?/?—?/3/12.**G.**
Don. 30/1—27/5/22.**G.**
Don. 8/3—26/5/23.**H.**
Don. 23/1—4/4/25.**G.**
Don. 14/9—13/10/25.**H.**
Don. 7/6—1/10/26.**G.**
Don. 7/11—21/12/28.**G.**
Don. 13/8—24/9/32.**G.**
Don. 30/11—21/12/35.**G.**
Don. 20/7—3/8/40.**G.**
Don. 5—26/2/44.**G.**
Don. 21/12/47—22/1/48.**G.**
Don. 10—21/10/49.**C/L.**
Push & pull fitted.
Don. 19/12/50—19/1/51.**G.**
Don. 6/11—11/12/52.**G.**
Don. 22/4—5/5/54.**C/L.**
Don. 12—26/10/54.**C/L.**
Don. 27/1/55. *Not repaired.*

BOILERS:
1465.
1512 3/12.
348 27/5/22.
7039 26/5/23.
6986 1/10/26.
8158 21/12/35.
8146 3/8/40.
21816 19/1/51.
21886 11/12/52.

SHEDS:
Hatfield *at* 10/1/23.
Boston 26/1/27.
Annesley 13/11/49.
Yarmouth 23/12/51.
Lowestoft 18/7/54.
Stratford 19/9/54.
Yarmouth 31/10/54.

RENUMBERED:
4537 4/4/25.
7387 2/6/46.

E**7387** 22/1/48.
67387 21/10/49.

CONDEMNED: 7/2/55.
Cut up at Doncaster.

4538

Doncaster 1024.

To traffic 12/1903.
.
REPAIRS:
Don. ?/?—?/6/10.**G.**
Don. 15/7—28/10/22.**G.**
Don. 11/5—11/7/25.**G.**
Don. 23/8—3/10/28.**G.**
Don. 9/8—20/9/30.**G.**
Don. 15/7—5/8/33.**G.**
Don. 23/5—16/6/36.**G.**
Don. 3—24/12/38.**G.**
Don. 25/7—1/8/42.**G.**
Don. 4—11/12/43.**L.**
Don. 9/6—21/7/45.**G.**
Don. 12/1/46.**L.**
Don. 9/6/48. *Not repaired.*

BOILERS:
1464.
1501 6/10.
8144 3/10/28.
8761 16/6/36.
8557 1/8/42.

SHEDS:
Copley Hill.
Ardsley 10/12/37.
Trafford Park 30/3/40.
Northwich 10/5/40.
Trafford Park 17/12/41.
Gorton 8/3/42.
Trafford Park 6/11/42.
Copley Hill 23/2/47.

RENUMBERED:
4538 11/7/25.
7388 29/6/46.

CONDEMNED: 6/7/48.
Cut up at Doncaster.

4539

Doncaster 1025.

To traffic 1/1904.

REPAIRS:
Don. ?/?—?/3/10.**G.**
Don. ?/?—?/10/21.**G.**
Don. 23/6—12/8/22.**G.**
Don. 21/4—16/7/25.**G.**
Don. 31/3—17/8/27.**G.**

4539 cont./
Don. 7/9—12/10/29.**G.**
Don. 23/7—13/8/32.**G.**
Don. 10/8—21/9/35.**G.**
Don. 18/11—9/12/39.**G.**
Don. 16/5—6/6/42.**G.**
Don. 30/1—6/2/43.**L.**
Don. 19/8—9/9/44.**G.**
Don. 1—22/9/45.**L.**
Don. 9/11—7/12/46.**G.**
Don. 18/9—21/10/49.**G.**
Don. 22/9—17/10/52.**G.**
Don. 15/4/55. *Not repaired.*

BOILERS:
1477.
1507 3/10.
349 10/21.
1138 16/7/25.
6837 17/8/27.
8306 12/10/29.
8441 9/9/44.
21883 17/10/52.

SHEDS:
Ardsley.
Bradford 22/11/30.
Louth 8/6/37.
Lincoln 27/8/50.
Cambridge 10/12/50.
New England 29/4/51.
Botanic Gardens 27/3/55.

RENUMBERED:
4539 16/7/25.
7389 29/9/46.
67389 21/10/49.

CONDEMNED: 15/4/55.
Cut up at Doncaster.

_____

4540

Doncaster 1026.

To traffic 12/1903.

REPAIRS:
Don. 24/11/19—14/2/20.**G.**
Don. 23/4—11/8/23.**G.**
Don. 3/11/24—21/2/25.**G.**
After collision on 14/10/24.
Don. 14/9—26/11/27.**G.**
Don. 8/2—8/3/30.**G.**
Don. 24/9—22/10/32.**G.**
Don. 16/3—13/4/40.**G.**
Don. 25/3—15/4/44.**G.**
Don. 7/8—26/9/47.**G.**
Don. 26/7—25/8/50.**G.**
Don. 4/6/53. *Not repaired.*

BOILERS:
1479.
6838 14/2/20.

8327 8/3/30.
10573 25/8/50.

SHEDS:
Bradford.
Copley Hill 30/3/32.
New England 20/4/37.
Boston 24/6/40.
New England 22/8/40.

RENUMBERED:
4540 21/2/25.
7390 15/10/46.
67390 25/8/50.

CONDEMNED: 15/6/53.
Cut up at Doncaster.

_____

4541

Doncaster 1155.

To traffic 6/1907.

REPAIRS:
Don. ?/?—?/6/21.**G.**
Don. 23/5—30/9/22.**G.**
Don. 23/1—18/4/25.**G.**
Don. 26/5—30/9/27.**G.**
Don. 1—22/2/30.**G.**
Don. 19/11—10/12/32.**G.**
Don. 16/2—2/3/35.**G.**
Don. 4—25/5/35.**H.**
Don. 15/5—5/6/37.**G.**
Don. 2—16/3/40.**G.**
Don. 5—26/9/42.**G.**
Don. 23/9—7/10/44.**G.**
Don. 11/4—10/5/47.**G.**
Don. 21/3—8/4/49.**G.**
Don. 5/7—2/8/51.**G.**
Don. 30/8—25/9/53.**G.**
Don. 10/1/58. *Not repaired.*

BOILERS:
6835
6839 6/21.
7815 30/9/27.
8557 10/12/32.
8548 2/3/35.
8146 5/6/37.
8164 16/3/40.
7817 26/9/42.
8269 *(exJ50 8970)* 10/5/47.
21832 2/8/51.
21943 25/9/53.

SHEDS:
Hatfield *at* 10/1/23.
Doncaster 30/9/27.
Colwick 10/7/29.
Botanic Gardens 14/5/30.
Grantham 27/3/55.

RENUMBERED:
4541 18/4/25.
7391 17/11/46.
67391 8/4/49.

CONDEMNED: 10/1/58.
Cut up at Doncaster.

_____

4542

Doncaster 1156.

To traffic 6/1907.

REPAIRS:
Don. ?/?—?/4/15.**G.**
Don. 6/5—10/7/20.**G.**
Don. 12/10/23—15/2/24.**G.**
Don. 22/3—21/8/26.**G.**
Don. 21/9—19/10/28.**G.**
Don. 28/2—28/3/31.**G.**
Don. 27/5—17/6/33.**G.**
Don. 1—22/6/35.**G.**
Don. 20/3—10/4/37.**G.**
Don. 17/2—9/3/40.**G.**
Don. 6/3—3/4/43.**G.**
Don. 30/10—13/11/43.**L.**
Don. 7/7—4/8/45.**H.**
Don. 2/7—23/8/47.**G.**
Don. 11/4—6/5/49.**G.**
Don. 30/4—25/5/51.**G.**
Don. 2—15/1/52.**C/L.**
Don. 16—31/10/52.**C/L.**
Don. 18/6—21/7/53.**G.**
Don. 7—19/1/54.**C/L.**
Don. 25/8—3/9/54.**C/L.**
Don. 19/10/56. *Not repaired.*

BOILERS:
6837.
1469 4/15.
1479 10/7/20.
8157 19/10/28.
7932 22/6/35.
8158 *(ex 4537)* 3/4/43.
8307 *(exJ50 8913)* 23/8/47.
21913 *(new)* 25/5/51.
21808 21/7/53.

SHEDS:
Ardsley.
Lincoln *by* 12/28.
Botanic Gardens 13/4/31.
New England 27/3/55.

RENUMBERED:
4542 15/2/24.
7392 12/10/46.
67392 6/5/49.

CONDEMNED: 19/10/56.
Cut up at Doncaster.

_____

4543

Doncaster 1157.

To traffic 6/1907.

REPAIRS:
Don. ?/?—?/3/20.**G.**
Don. 27/11/22—24/2/23.**G.**
Don. 4/11/25—20/2/26.**G.**
Don. 12/6—25/9/28.**G.**
Don. 23/5—13/6/31.**G.**
Don. 25/3—29/4/33.**G.**
Don. 5—26/10/35.**G.**
Don. 22—29/1/38.**G.**
Don. 17/12/38—21/1/39.**L.**
Don. 6—27/4/40.**G.**
Don. 9/5—6/6/42.**G.**
Don. 1—22/7/44.**G.**
Don. 7/9—5/10/46.**H.**
Don. 11/12/48—8/1/49.**G.**
Don. 16/2—15/3/51.**G.**
Don. 13/4/53. *Not repaired.*

BOILERS:
6836.
1630 3/20.
8145 25/9/28.
8508 13/6/31.
7924 26/10/35.
7817 29/1/38.
8143 27/4/40.
8766 6/6/42.
8318 *(ex 7364)* 8/1/49.
21909 *(new)* 15/3/51.

SHEDS:
Bradford.
Botanic Gardens 24/6/31.

RENUMBERED:
4543 20/2/26.
7393 1/12/46.
67393 7/1/49.

CONDEMNED: 20/4/53.
Cut up at Doncaster.

_____

4544

Doncaster 1158.

To traffic 7/1907.

REPAIRS:
Don. ?/?—?/9/18.**G.**
Don. 20/8—23/10/20.**G.**
Don. 2/1—12/4/24.**G.**
Don. 26/5—18/8/27.**G.**
Don. 11/5—15/6/29.**G.**
Don. 16/1—20/2/32.**G.**
Don. 10—31/12/32.**L.**
Don. 19/1—9/2/35.**G.**
Don. 18—31/12/37.**G.**

The other engine to get the tablet exchanger was No.4015 in May 1937. Note that the top lamp iron has been moved on to the door.

(right) M&GN tablet apparatus was fitted on both sides of the C12 engines. Note that 4015 had four bunker rails and they had plating behind.

(below) In the same batch, No.4014 kept the original two rails but No.4020 had three (*see* page 9, top) and in the 1930's both were fitted with plating behind the rails. Copley Hill.

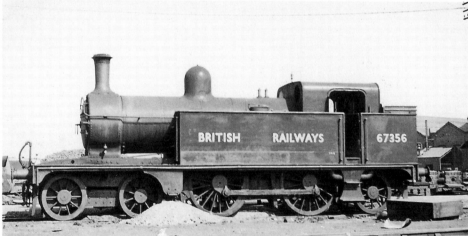

(above) **Ex works on Wednesday 31st December 1947, No.7374 had been fitted with vacuum controlled push and pull apparatus taken from F2 class, for use on the Finsbury Park - Alexandra Palace shuttle service.**

(left) **No.67356 was ex works on 12th January 1949 and returned to Copley Hill shed. Note it still had only the two coal rails from when it was No.1018.**

From 23rd April to 5th May 1949 No.67356 was back in Doncaster works to have vacuum controlled push and pull apparatus fitted and on 8th May 1949 it was transferred to King's Cross shed to join No.7374 on the Alexandra Palace service. Three more C12's were fitted in 1949 with push and pull gear, Nos.67363 (18th February), 67386 (2nd March), 67387 (21st October), initially for use at Annesley and Ardsley - *see* **pages 41, middle and 43, top. When No.67387 was withdrawn, its gear was transferred to No.67366, ex works 14th April 1955.**

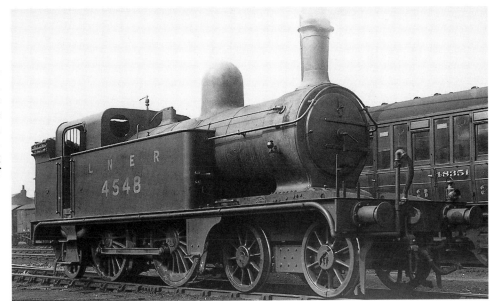

Some engines in the London Area - No.4548 remained at Hatfield shed until 24th December 1926 - were fitted with extra and also double height lamp irons to carry Southern Railway codes for through working. Lamp brackets in corresponding positions were fitted on the back of the bunker (*see* page 10, top).

(right) No.4016 worked in the G.E. section from March 1933 to November 1938 and for some reason had been fitted with two extra lamp irons although it was not a London Area engine at any time. It was one of the C12's which kept the original two coal rails.

(below) Although No.1020 was never in either the London or Nottingham Areas, where destination boards were used, this 30th June 1923 illustration shows brackets fitted for them on its smokebox door. It probably had an exchange of doors at a previous repair, ex works on 26th November 1921.

Only the ten engines built in 1907, Nos.4541 to 4550, got fluted coupling rods when they were new, and some managed to keep that type. These ten also differed in having a single footstep on the front of the side tanks instead of two on the earlier engines.

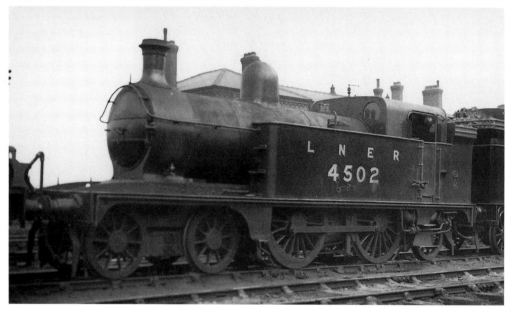

The fifty earlier engines all had plain coupling rods and changes to fluted type were rare although they did occur (*see* pages 30, bottom; 40, top and 41, top). Doncaster shed.

No.4541 had its condensing apparatus removed at a shed and not by Doncaster works. In the process the vent pipe at the rear of each tank was left in place for some years, at least to March 1940, but they had gone by May 1947. It was the only one so treated.

4544 cont./
Don. 4—18/5/40.**G.**
Don. 13/6—11/7/42.**G.**
Don. 1—29/4/44.**G.**
Don. 1/6—20/7/46.**G.**
Don. 19/7—13/8/48.**G.**
Don. 28/3—20/4/51.**G.**
Don. 26/11—15/12/52.**C/L.**
Don. 3—27/11/53.**G.**
Don. 12—23/8/54.**C/L.**
Don. 16/6/58. *Not repaired.*

BOILERS:
6838.
6844 9/18.
7005 15/6/29.
8548 20/2/32.
7951 9/2/35.
8675 31/12/37.
8515 18/5/40.
9640 *(new)* 20/7/46.
21908 *(new)* 20/4/51.
21800 27/11/53.

SHEDS:
Bradford.
Doncaster *after* 5/24.
Bradford 6/12/26.
Botanic Gardens 24/2/32.
New England 27/3/55.

RENUMBERED:
4544 12/4/24.
7394 12/10/46.
67394 13/8/48.

CONDEMNED: 16/6/58.
Cut up at Doncaster.

4545

Doncaster 1159.

To traffic 7/1907.

REPAIRS:
Don. 4/11/20—12/3/21.**G.**
Don. 8/6—5/8/22.**L.**
Don. 29/10/23—31/1/24.**G.**
Don. 15/3—4/6/27.**G.**
Don. 21/12/29—18/1/30.**G.**
Don. 14/5—4/6/32.**G.**
Don. 10—31/12/32.**L.**
Don. 28/7—18/8/34.**G.**
Don. 2—16/5/36.**G.**
Don. 23/7—20/8/38.**G.**
Don. 13/7—3/8/40.**G.**
Don. 14/11—5/12/42.**G.**
Don. 17/4—8/5/43.**L.**
Don. 9/12/44—6/1/45.**G.**
Don. 24/8—28/9/46.**G.**
Don. 27/12/47—17/1/48.**L.**
Don. 22/12/48—15/1/49.**G.**
Don. 30/1—20/2/51.**G.**

Don. 16/5—6/6/51.**C/L.**
Don. 10—27/7/51.**C/L.**
Don. 29/8—26/9/51.**C/L.**
Don. 8/10—5/11/53.**G.**
Don. 2—16/12/55.**C/L.**

BOILERS:
6839.
6841 12/3/21.
1138 4/6/27.
8320 18/1/30.
8765 16/5/36.
7951 20/8/38.
9642 *(new)* 28/9/46.
21904 *(new)* 20/2/51.
21945 5/11/53.

SHEDS:
Bradford.
Botanic Gardens 16/5/30.
Bury St Edmunds. 27/3/55.
Cambridge 8/1/56.

RENUMBERED:
1545N 31/1/24.
4545 4/6/27.
7395 28/9/46.
67395 14/1/49.

CONDEMNED: 16/3/57.
Cut up at Doncaster.

4546

Doncaster 1160.

To traffic 7/1907.

REPAIRS:
Don. ?/?—?/10/15.**G.**
Don. ?/?—?/11/20.**G.**
Don. 5/2—12/5/23.**G.**
Don. 16/10/25—5/1/26.**G.**
Don. 4/10—29/12/26.**L.**
Don. 15/11—29/12/28.**G.**
Don. 31/1—28/2/31.**G.**
Don. 22/10—19/11/32.**G.**
Don. 25/11—3/12/32.**L.**
Don. 18/8—22/9/34.**G.**
Don. 25/7—15/8/36.**G.**
Don. 16/7—13/8/38.**G.**
Don. 24/8—5/10/40.**G.**
Don. 23/1—13/2/43.**G.**
Don. 22—29/1/44.**L.**
Don. 6/1—17/2/45.**G.**
Don. 8—15/9/45.**L.**
Don. 7/6/47. *Not repaired.*

BOILERS:
6840.
6841 10/15.
1623 11/20.
8485 28/2/31.
8151 15/8/36.

8767 13/8/38.

SHEDS:
Bradford.
Botanic Gardens 2/3/31.

RENUMBERED:
4546 27/2/25.
7396 3/11/46.

CONDEMNED: 23/6/47.
Cut up at Doncaster.

4547

Doncaster 1161.

To traffic 7/1907.

REPAIRS:
Don. ?/?—?/11/14.**G.**
Don. 25/2—30/9/22.**G.**
Don. 25/9—5/12/25.**G.**
Don. 21/6—18/8/28.**G.**
Don. 21/3—18/4/31.**G.**
Don. 18/3—8/4/33.**G.**
Don. 22/12/34—12/1/35.**G.**
Don. 17—31/10/36.**G.**
Don. 29/4—3/6/39.**G.**
Don. 29/3—19/4/41.**G.**
Don. 28/2—21/3/42.**L.**
Don. 27/2—27/3/43.**G.**
Don. 9/6—14/7/45.**G.**
Don. 11/8—8/9/45.**L.**
Don. 24/12/47—26/1/48.**G.**
Don. 31/1—24/3/50.**G.**
Don. 16/4—9/5/52.**G.**
Don. 27/10/52.**N/C.**
Don. 28/1—12/2/53.**C/L.**
Don. 8—14/7/53.**N/C.**
Don. 17/5—11/6/54.**G.**
Don. 25/11—8/12/55.**C/L.**
Don. 13/6—10/7/56.**C/L.**
Don. 6/12/58. *Not repaired.*

BOILERS:
6841.
1164 11/14.
8490 18/4/31.
8770 31/10/36.
8767 *(ex 7396)* 26/1/48.
21865 9/5/52.
21844 11/6/54.

SHEDS:
Bradford.
Botanic Gardens 22/4/31.
Bury St Edmunds. 27/3/55.
Cambridge 1/1/56.
Spital Bridge 24/3/57.
Grantham 7/7/57.

RENUMBERED:
4547 5/12/25.

7397 3/11/46.
E**7397** 26/1/48.
67397 24/3/50.

CONDEMNED: 6/12/58.
Cut up at Doncaster.

4548

Doncaster 1162.

To traffic 7/1907.

REPAIRS:
Don. ?/?—?/1/20.**G.**
Don. 19/4—23/9/22.**G.**
Don. 21/12/23—29/3/24.**G.**
Don. 6/11/24—10/1/25.**G.**
Don. 17—31/1/25.**L.**
Don. 15/9—16/12/26.**G.**
Don. 16/2—3/5/28.**G.**
Don. 28/6—2/8/30.**G.**
Don. 3—24/6/33.**G.**
Don. 4/2—18/3/39.**G.**
Don. 12/6—24/7/43.**G.**
Don. 2/2—2/3/46.**G.**
Don. 24/4—28/5/48.**G.**
Don. 11/4—7/5/51.**G.**
Don. 24/5—28/6/54.**G.**
Don. 14/5/55.**N/C.**
Don. 4/11/58. *Not repaired.*

In store:
23/6/33—4/12/36.
17/12/36—22/4/37.
14/4/39—8/3/40.

BOILERS:
6842.
1508 1/20.
1632 29/3/24.
8441 2/8/30.
8143 24/7/43.
21911 *(new)* 7/5/51.
21836 28/6/54.

SHEDS:
Hatfield.
Colwick 24/12/26.
Annesley 22/3/30.
Colwick 25/4/30.
Langwith Jct. 11/3/31.
Colwick 25/3/31.
Trafford Park 16/10/41.
Gorton 8/3/42.
Langwith Jct. 20/7/42.
Louth 21/7/44.
Immingham 2/12/56.
New England 20/1/57.

RENUMBERED:
4548 29/3/24.
7398 20/10/46.
67398 28/5/48.

4548 cont./
CONDEMNED: 4/11/58.
Cut up at Doncaster.

_____

4549

Doncaster 1163.

To traffic 7/1907.

REPAIRS:
Don. ?/?—?/7/16.**G.**
Don. 4/11/20—12/3/21.**G.**
Don. 26/9—31/12/24.**G.**
Don. 4/10/26—11/2/27.**G.**
Don. 4/5—8/6/29.**G.**
Don. 14/11—12/12/31.**G.**
Don. 17/6—8/7/33.**G.**
Don. 9—23/3/35.**G.**
Don. 13/11—4/12/37.**G.**
Don. 12—19/3/38.**L.**
Don. 1—15/6/40.**G.**
Don. 30/5—27/6/42.**G.**
Don. 19/2—11/3/44.**G.**
Don. 4/8—8/9/45.**G.**
Don. 26—30/11/46.**L.**
Don. 11/10—15/11/47.**G.**
Don. 27/9/49. *Not repaired.*

BOILERS:
6843.
1525 7/16.
7039 11/2/27.
8511 12/12/31.
7821 23/3/35.
8490 4/12/37.
8326 *(exJ4 4120)* 15/11/47.

SHEDS:
Bradford.
Botanic Gardens 26/12/31.

RENUMBERED:
4549 31/12/24.
7399 3/11/46.

CONDEMNED: 28/11/49.
Cut up at Doncaster.

_____

4550

Doncaster 1164.

To traffic 8/1907.

REPAIRS:
Don. ?/?—?/6/18.**G.**
Don. 25/9—23/12/22.**G.**
Don. 1/5—1/8/25.**G.**
Don. 27/9—8/12/27.**G.**
Don. 30/11—28/12/29.**G.**
Don. 27/5—1/7/33.**G.**
Don. 21/3—11/4/36.**G.**

BOILERS:
6844.
1520 6/18.
1652 1/8/25.
8318 28/12/29.
8143 11/4/36.

SHEDS:
Hatfield *by* 10/4/23.
New England 27/1/27.
Botanic Gardens 27/9/30.

RENUMBERED:
4550 1/8/25.

CONDEMNED: 6/12/38.
Cut up at Doncaster.

Throughout, this class had vacuum brake only, both on engine and for the train brake. The ejector exhaust pipe was always through the boiler and the drainpipe, if fitted, was never visible. Doncaster shed.

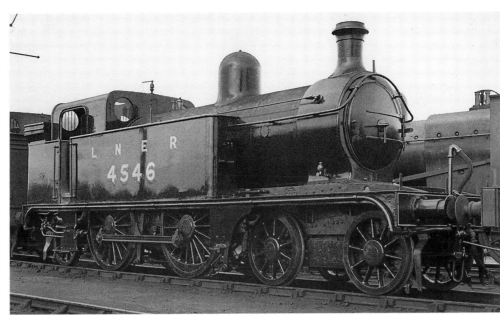

(right) **This boiler had been prepared for an engine with condensing apparatus as the clack box opening has been blanked off. It is probably the boiler built in 1906 which No.4546 carried from November 1920 to February 1931. Doncaster shed.**

(below) **During the 1914-1918 war the green livery was discarded and grey with single white lining was then used but it is fairly certain that all had been restored to green before Grouping. King's Cross shed.**

Standard livery when the LNER took over was green with a broad black and two narrow white lines. The tanks and bunker had panels with scalloped corners. No.1550 left works on 23rd December 1922 in this livery with the number on the bunker but with plain tanks. No.1516 was the last with green; it went to works on 5th October 1925.

The LNER choice of livery for the C12's was black with single red lining and 12in. shaded transfer numbers displayed on the tank side, until mid-June 1923 the 7$\frac{1}{2}$in. company initials included the ampersand. To September 1923 LNER and the original number was put on No.1015 (28th July),1540 (11th August), 1019 (20th August), 1017 (25th August),1521 (1st September). Note the collar on the vacuum pipe showing G.N.R. load Class M. Nottingham (Victoria).

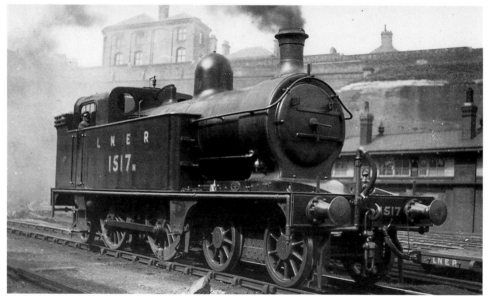

From September 1923 to mid February 1924, area suffix N was added to the number on the tank but not on the buffer beam number. Eight were so treated: 1013 (13th October 1923), 1517 (1st December 1923), 1526 (5th January 1924), 1525 (12th January 1924), 1530 (19th January 1924), 1535 (19th January 1924), 1545 (31st January 1924) and 1509 (2nd February 1924). Nottingham (Victoria).

Beginning with No.4542, ex works on 15th February 1924 there was then stability in numbering and painting until during the war and after the death of Gresley. The word Class was not put on buffer beam by Doncaster until the first week of March 1938, No.4534 getting it when ex works 9th July 1938.

From June 1942 only NE was used, until January 1946. but in 12in. instead of 7½in. letters. The red lining had been stopped from November 1941 and was never resumed. No.4520 was NE when ex works on 23rd December 1944 and never had LNER restored.

No.4009ᴀ was one of the first to get LNER again; it was ex works on 16th February 1946. Note that it had the duplicate list number also on the buffer beam. No.1009 had the A added during August 1921 when a new 2-6-0 took that number.

The 1946 renumbering entailed the C12's gaining Nos.7350 to 7399 and these took a variety of forms according to facilities available. No.4537 became 7387 on Sunday 2nd June 1946 by stencilling at Boston shed.

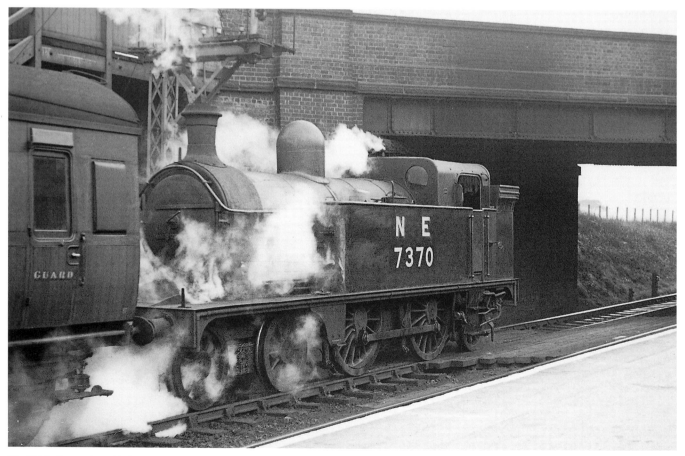

No.4513 changed to 7370 on Saturday 5th October 1946 at Trafford Park shed and the use of 12in. shaded transfers indicates it was done by a Gorton works painter.

(above) **No.4543 became 7393 on Sunday 1st December 1946 at Hull Botanic Gardens shed and a local painter tried to match the style he blacked out except for the shading. No.4543 had regained LNER when ex works on 5th October 1946.**

(right) **No.4520 was a Cambridge engine (*see also* page 37, top), and was sub-shedded at Saffron Walden. It was renumbered 7375 on Tuesday 24th September 1946 by a local painter, the 9½in. deep numbers being quite unusual. The other three Cambridge engines were all done on Sundays.**

Another Cambridge engine, No.4509 became 7367 on Sunday 26th May 1946 but went for general repair on 3rd August 1946. Ex Doncaster on 31st August, it had LNER and its number applied properly in shaded transfers. Doncaster shed.

From April 1947, Doncaster ceased to use transfers on the C12 class and changed to yellow painted and unshaded Gill sans letters and numbers but with modified 6 and 9. During 1947 ten of the class were put into this style and one got it in 1948: 7351 (12th May), 7364 (2nd August), 7365 (3rd June), 7368 (28th July), 7374 (31st December), 7384 (25th May), 7390 (26th September), 7391 (10th May), 7392 (23rd August) and 7399 (15th November), whilst No.7354 was done on 11th January 1948.

From mid-January to mid-March 1948, four C12 were ex works with BRITISH RAILWAYS lettering and the regional prefix E to the numbers: E7369 (16th January), E7387 (22nd January), E7397 (26th January), E7352 (27th February). Manchester Central.

The next variation was the substitution of the E by a 6 with the number still on the front buffer beam and three acquired this style, all during 1948: Nos.67366 (2nd April), 67360 (6th May) and 67398 (28th May).

(below) Another change took place in July 1948 when a cast number plate was fitted on the smokebox door supplanting the painted numbers on the buffer beam. This style using the modified 6 and 9 continued for six months and was applied on unlined black. 1948:- 67375 (23rd July), 67352 (28th July), 67354 (31st July), 67394 (13th August), 67364 (3rd September), 67386 (24th September), 67371 (15th October), 67350 (29th October), 67380 (29th October), 67373 (27th November), 67384 (28th December); 1949:- 67393 (7th January) 67356 (12th January), 67395 (14th January), 67381 (27th January). One more, 67363 (18th February 1949) got a smokebox plate with the modified 6 but had the correct Gill sans 6 on its bunker.

Two more got unlined black and BRITISH RAILWAYS, with the correct 6 and 9 both on the smokebox plate and the bunker. These were 67391 on 8th April 1949, and 67392 on 6th May 1949.

By the next painting, the first emblem had superseded British Railways and red, cream and grey lining had been sanctioned. Starting with 67389 (21st October 1949) and 67379 (4th November 1949), no less than thirty-six survived to get this livery.

The 1946 renumbering ended the duplicate list A because No.4009A became No.7350 on 22nd December 1946. Boston.

The last C12 to have a general repair was No.67363, ex works on 22nd December 1956, and it retained the smokebox number plate with the LNER modified 6.

In normal service no C12 survived to get the second BR emblem introduced in 1957 but No.67352 was specially cleaned and painted by King's Cross shed to appear in an exhibition of rolling stock at Noel Park Goods Yard, Wood Green on 12th to 14th September 1958. A pair of new emblem transfers was obtained and applied to it.

Gorton built eight in 1903 and nineteen more during 1904 and 1905 and these also were without superheater at Grouping. Note that these had no step fitted on the bunker.

The remaining engine, No.18 built at Gorton in 1904, had been fitted in July 1915 with a longer smokebox, fifteen element superheater and a Wakefield mechanical lubricator. Trafford Park.

CLASS C 13

6055

Vulcan 1874

To traffic 3/1903

REPAIRS:
Gor. 16/9—7/10/11.**G**.
Gor. 17/9—29/10/21.**G**.
Gor. 3/11/23—2/2/24.**G**.
Gor. 19/12/25—6/3/26.**G**.
Superheated boiler fitted.
Altered to 13ft gauge.
Gor. 11/2—24/3/28.**G**.
Gor. 21/12/29—25/1/30.**G**.
Gor. 23/7—6/8/32.**G**.
Gor. 2—23/6/34.**G**.
Over 13ft gauge.
Gor. 14—28/3/36.**G**.
Altered to 13ft gauge.
Fountain lub. to axles.
Gor. 5—26/2/38.**G**.
Gor. 9—30/12/39.**G**.
Gor. 28/9—19/10/40.**L**.
Don. 19/8—6/9/41.**L**.
Gor. 21/2—21/3/42.**G**.
Gor. 31/10—7/11/42.**L**.
Gor. 2—13/11/43.**G**.
Gor. 7—14/4/45.**L**.
Gor. 8—29/6/46.**G**.
Gor. 24/1—28/2/48.**G**.
Gor. 1—22/10/49.**G**.
Gor. 15/9—6/10/51.**G**.
Gor. 14/2—7/3/53.**G**.
Gor. 29/1—5/3/55.**C/L**.

BOILERS:
344.
226 *(new)* 7/10/11.
662 *(sup.new)* 6/3/26.
285 *(ex5115)* 6/8/32.
904 *(exC14 6122)* 23/6/34.
348 *(ex5191)* 28/3/36.
1595 *(ex5178)* 26/2/38.
979 *(D6 5874)* 30/12/39.
688 *(C14 6128)* 13/11/43.
661 *(ex6062)* 29/6/46.
350 *(ex7432)* 28/2/48.
4511 *(67414)* 22/10/49.
22933 *(new)* 6/10/51.
22919 *(ex67435)* 7/3/53.

SHEDS:
Sheffield 7/7/22.
Trafford Park 13/5/30.
Northwich 23/7/30.
Trafford Park 24/8/32.
Northwich 9/9/32.
Trafford Park 28/3/36.
Gorton 7/1/42.

Chester 27/3/47.
Wrexham 22/10/55.

RENUMBERED:
6055 2/2/24.
7400 21/9/46.
ᴇ7400 28/2/48.
67400 5/3/49.

CONDEMNED: 29/12/56.
Cut up at Doncaster.

6056

Vulcan 1875.

To traffic 3/1903.

REPAIRS:
Gor. 10/10—14/11/14.**G**.
Gor. 24/12/21—4/2/22.**G**.
Gor. 12/1—8/3/24.**G**.
Gor. 16/10/26—5/2/27.**G**.
Superheated boiler fitted.
Altered to 13ft gauge.
Gor. 8/12/28—26/1/29.**G**.
Gor. 6/9—18/10/30.**G**.
Gor. 21/5—4/6/32.**G**.
Gor. 30/12/33—20/1/34.**G**.
Gor. 20/6—11/7/36.**G**.
Fountain lub. to axles.
Gor. 9—23/7/38.**G**.
Gor. 6—20/7/40.**G**.
Gor. 29/4—15/5/43.**G**.
Gor. 3—26/10/44.**G**.
Gor. 28/12/46—18/1/47.**G**.
Gor. 20/3—24/4/48.**G**.
Gor. 17/9—8/1049.**G**.
Gor. 29/4—6/5/50.**C/L**.
After collision.
Gor. 11—25/8/51.**H/I**.
Gor. 12—26/9/53.**G**.

BOILERS:
345.
358 *(ex28)* 14/11/14.
697 *(sup.new)* 5/2/27.
757 *(D6 5270)* 4/6/32.
349 *(ex5357)* 20/1/34.
329 *(ex5310)* 11/7/36.
688 *(D6 5879)* 23/7/38.
740 *(ex5114)* 20/7/40.
976 *(ex5193)* 15/5/43.
729 *(ex5188)* 26/10/44.
746 *(ex7415)* 18/1/47.
975 *(ex7421)* 8/10/49.
975 reno. 22929 25/8/51.
22910 *(ex67404)* 26/9/53.

SHEDS:
Sheffield .
Woodford 9/4/25.
Sheffield 20/10/26.
Barnsley 23/2/34.
Sheffield 25/10/35.
Retford 12/10/36.
Gorton 7/5/37.
Wrexham 10/8/38.
Northwich 9/1/39.
Gorton 1/11/39.
Ardsley 24/8/41.
Bradford 20/9/41.
Gorton 2/6/42.

RENUMBERED:
6056 8/3/24.
7401 20/10/46.
67401 24/4/48.

CONDEMNED: 28/12/55.
Into Dar. for cut up 25/1/56.

6057

Vulcan 1876.

To traffic 4/1903.

REPAIRS:
Gor. 3/5—28/6/13.**G**.
Gor. 13/11—24/12/20.**G**.
Gor. 20/1—24/2/23.**G**.
Gor. 31/1—5/9/25.**G**.
Gor. 16/6—21/7/28.**G**.
Gor. 1/8—9/9/31.**G**.
Gor. 3/9—1/10/32.**G**.
Superheated boiler fitted.
Gor. 2—9/2/35.**G**.
Altered to 13ft gauge.
Fountain lub. to axles.
Gor. 25/1—8/2/36.**G**.
Gor. 1—15/1/38.**G**.
Gor. 17/2—16/3/40.**G**.
Gor. 26/2—4/4/42.**G**.
Gor. 18/12/43—8/1/44.**G**.
Gor. 23/6—21/7/45.**G**.
Gor. 29/3—3/5/47.**G**.
Gor. 17/9—8/10/49.**G**.
Gor. 24/11—22/12/51.**H/I**.
Gor. 3—17/1/53.**C/L**.
Gor. 7/8/54. *Not repaired.*

BOILERS:
346.
353 *(ex1064)* 28/6/13.
456 *(exD6 5871)* 5/9/25.
637 *(sup.exD6 5871)* 1/10/32.
4504 *(new)* 9/2/35.

740 *(ex6064)* 8/2/36.
330 *(ex6062)* 15/1/38.
4504 *(ex5454)* 16/3/40.
663 *(ex5359)* 8/1/44.
976 *(ex6056)* 21/7/45.
686 *(ex7421)* 3/5/47.
4512 *(exᴇ7403)* 8/10/49.
4512 reno. 22936 22/12/51.

SHEDS:
Sheffield 4/3/21.
Staveley 3/11/30.
Sheffield 16/2/31.
Woodford 14/11/31.
Chester 5/8/32.
Trafford Park 5/10/32.
Northwich 10/2/36.
Trafford Park 9/10/36.
Gorton 7/1/42.
Wrexham 9/7/42.
Gorton 13/10/46.

RENUMBERED:
6057 5/9/25.
7402 28/7/46.
67402 8/10/49.

CONDEMNED: 16/8/54.
Into Don. for cut up 14/9/54.

6058

Vulcan 1877.

To traffic 4/1903.

REPAIRS:
Gor. 4/5—29/6/12.**G**.
Gor. 9/10—4/12/20.**G**.
Gor. 5/5—1/12/23.**G**.
Gor. 30/1—24/4/26.**G**.
Gor. 9/3—20/4/29.**G**.
Gor. 1—29/8/31.**G**.
Superheated boiler fitted.
Altered to 13ft gauge.
Gor. 24/3—21/4/34.**G**.
Gor. 1—15/8/36.**G**.
Fountain lub. to axles.
Gor. 23/7—6/8/38.**G**.
Gor. 5/4—3/5/41.**G**.
Gor. 13/3—3/4/43.**G**.
Gor. 9—30/12/44.**G**.
Gor. 9/11—14/12/46.**G**.
Gor. 13/12/47—24/1/48.**L**.
Gor. 28/5—25/6/49.**G**.
Gor.17/2—17/3/51.**H/I**.
Gor. 2—9/8/52.**C/L**.
Gor. 4/10—1/11/52.**G**.

45

From February 1926 the other thirty-nine engines had a superheater put in but No.5453 the last C13 fitted to complete the job, was not superheated until April 1935. Wrexham shed, April 1946.

Superheating needed a longer smokebox and pieces welding to the frame to suit. Apart from No.8, a Gresley anti-vacuum valve was used, and at first was fitted at the end of the header.

There was no fixed position for the anti-vacuum valve as it could be at either end of the header.

There were even instances where an anti-vacuum valve was fitted to both ends of the header, No.5002 being one example. Manchester Central.

This class could use older boilers from D6 class which had tall domes and fifteen instead of the normal eighteen element superheater.

6058 cont./
BOILERS:
  347.
  1008 *(ex20)* 29/6/12.
  161 *(new)* 1/12/23.
  350 *(sup.new)* 29/8/31.
  365 *(new)* 21/4/34.
  372 *(ex5171)* 15/8/36.
  329 *(ex6056)* 6/8/38.
  4501 *(ex5191)* 3/5/41.
  755 *(ex5171)* 3/4/43.
  971 *(ex5114)* 30/12/44.
  4512 *(ex7425)* 14/12/46
  742 *(ex67425)* 25/6/49.
  742 reno. 22915 17/3/51.
  22913 *(ex67409)* 1/11/52.

SHEDS:
  Retford 28/7/22.
  Sheffield 12/5/29.
  Staveley 28/12/29.
  Sheffield 25/7/31.
  Staveley 16/9/31.
  Annesley 16/5/39.
  Colwick 28/1/40.
  Gorton 30/4/42.

RENUMBERED:
  1058c 8/12/23.
  6058 24/4/26.
  7403 14/12/46.
  E7403 24/1/48.
  67403 25/6/49.

CONDEMNED: 20/4/55.
Into Gor. for cut up 23/4/55.

_____

6059

Vulcan 1878.

To traffic 5/1903.

REPAIRS:
Gor. 28/10—16/12/11.**G.**
Gor. 25/10/13—17/1/14.**G.**
Gor. 18/11/22—5/1/23.**G.**
Gor. 17/1—4/7/25.**G.**
Gor. 14/1—10/3/28.**G.**
Gor. 19/7—16/8/30.**G.**
Gor. 15—29/7/33.**G.**
Superheated boiler fitted.
Altered to 13ft gauge.
Gor. 2—16/11/35.**G.**
Fountain lub. to axles.
Gor. 7—28/5/38.**G.**
Gor. 23/11—14/12/40.**G.**
Gor. 4—12/6/43.**G.**
Gor. 12—26/8/44.**L.**
Gor. 16/2—9/3/46.**G.**
Gor. 5—26/6/48.**G.**
Gor. 20/1—10/2/51.**H/I.**
Gor. 4/10/52.**L.**
Bunker patch fitted.

BOILERS:
  348.
  1022 *(ex114)* 16/12/11.
  1261 *(exC14 1131)* 17/1/14.
  330 *(sup.exC14 6123)* 29/7/33.
  691 *(ex5193)* 16/11/35.
  332 *(ex5179)* 28/5/38.
  4513 *(new)* 14/12/40.
  741 *(ex6064)* 12/6/43.
  4504 *(ex5357)* 9/3/46.
  979 *(ex7433)* 26/6/48.
  979 reno. 22910 10/2/51.

SHEDS:
  Sheffield 15/4/21.
  Retford 20/11/29.
  Sheffield 25/1/30.
  Barnsley 28/10/30.
  Sheffield 10/3/32.
  Barnsley 21/7/37.
  Sheffield 28/3/38.

RENUMBERED:
  6059 4/7/25.
  7404 7/7/46.
  67404 26/6/48.

CONDEMNED: 23/2/53.
Into Gor. for cut up 28/2/53.

_____

6060

Vulcan 1879.

To traffic 5/1903.

REPAIRS:
Gor. 1/11/13—14/2/14.**G.**
Gor. 9/7—6/8/21.**G.**
Gor. 9/6—18/8/23.**G.**
Gor. 13/6—12/12/25.**G.**
Gor. 19/11/27—14/1/28.**G.**
Gor. 30/11/29—11/1/30.**G.**
Superheated boiler fitted.
Altered to 13ft gauge.
Gor. 14/5—4/6/32.**G.**
Gor. 6—27/10/34.**G.**
Gor. 21/11—5/12/36.**G.**
Gor. 22/10—12/11/38.**G.**
Gor. 6/7—3/8/40.**G.**
Gor. 29/4—22/5/43.**G.**
Gor. 24/2—17/3/45.**G.**
Gor. 4/10—1/11/47.**G.**
Gor. 13—20/11/48.**L.**
Gor. 26/2—12/3/49.**C/H.**
Gor. 29/4—27/5/50.**G.**
Gor. 31/3—7/4/51.**C/L.**
Gor. 8—22/3/52.**C/L.**
After collision.
Gor. 4/10—1/11/52.**G.**

BOILERS:
  349.
  1260 *(exC14 1126)* 14/2/14.

979 *(sup.new)* 11/1/30.
  521 *(ex5020)* 5/12/36.
  975 *(ex5455)* 12/11/38.
  279 *(ex5455)* 3/8/40.
  4501 *(ex6058)* 22/5/43.
  329 *(ex5454)* 17/3/45.
  349 *(exC14 7450)* 1/11/47.
  744 *(ex67428)* 27/5/50.
  744 reno. 22917 7/4/51.
22901 *(ex67423)* 1/11/52.

SHEDS:
  Sheffield 20/8/20.
  Woodford 29/2/28.
  Sheffield 14/1/30.
  Trafford Park 5/6/30.
  Gorton 5/12/36.
  Trafford Park 11/10/41.
  Gorton 7/5/42.
  Northwich 5/5/46.
  Gorton 11/8/46.
  Chester 13/10/46.
  Gorton 24/1/47.

RENUMBERED:
  1060c 18/9/23.
  6060 12/12/25.
  7405 10/11/46.
  67405 20/11/48.

CONDEMNED: 2/5/55.
Into Gor. for cut up 7/5/55.

_____

6061

Vulcan 1880.

To traffic 5/1903.

REPAIRS:
Gor. 21/12/12—1/2/13.**G.**
Gor. 29/10/21—28/1/22.**G.**
Gor. 17/11/23—16/2/24.**G.**
Gor. 5/6—28/8/26.**G.**
Gor. 26/1—23/2/29.**G.**
Gor. 20/2—26/3/32.**G.**
Gor. 16/6—7/7/34.**G.**
Superheated boiler fitted.
Altered to 13ft gauge.
WPU gear removed.
Gor. 25/7—15/8/36.**G.**
Gor. 5—26/8/39.**G.**
Gor. 17/10—14/11/42.**G.**
Gor. 19/5—23/6/45.**G.**
Gor. 19—26/10/46.**L.**
Gor. 29/11—20/12/47.**G.**
Gor. 22/7—12/8/50.**G.**

BOILERS:
  350.
  1013 *(ex50)* 1/2/13.
  226 *(ex6055)* 28/8/26.
  521 *(ex5359)* 26/3/32.
  285 *(sup.)* 7/7/34.

686 *(ex spare)* 26/8/39.
  358 *(ex5188)* 14/11/42.
  4503 *(ex7423)* 20/12/47.
  743 *(ex67439)* 12/8/50.

SHEDS:
  Sheffield 30/6/03.
  Staveley 25/7/31.
  Sheffield 16/9/31.

RENUMBERED:
  6061 16/2/24.
  7406 7/7/46.
  67406 12/8/50.

CONDEMNED: 30/3/53.
Into Gor. for cut up 4/4/53.

_____

6062

Vulcan 1881.

To traffic 6/1903.

REPAIRS:
Gor. 2/1—6/2/15.**G.**
Gor. 21/1—11/3/22.**G.**
Gor. 1/3—24/5/24.**G.**
Gor. 19/6—25/9/26.**G.**
Gor. 23/6—28/7/28.**G.**
Gor. 20/12/30—31/1/31.**G.**
Gor. 26/8—23/9/33.**G.**
Superheated boiler fitted.
Altered to 13ft gauge.
Gor. 16/11—7/12/35.**G.**
Fountain lub. to axles.
Gor. 27/11—18/12/37.**G.**
Gor. 14—28/9/40.**G.**
Gor. 28/8—18/9/43.**G.**
Gor. 30/3—20/4/46.**G.**
Gor. 17/4—15/5/48.**G.**
Gor. 4—25/11/50.**G.**
Gor. 8/3—5/4/52.**C/H.**
Gor. 8—29/8/53.**G.**
Gor. 2—9/7/55.**C/L.**

BOILERS:
  351.
  359 *(ex188)* 6/2/15.
  363 *(ex spare)* 11/3/22.
  332 *(sup.ex5193)* 23/9/33.
  330 *(ex6059)* 7/12/35.
  741 *(exD6 5856)* 18/12/37.
  967 *(ex5310)* 28/9/40.
  661 *(ex6063)* 18/9/43.
  353 *(ex5456)* 20/4/46.
  4519 *(new)* 15/5/48.
22904 *(ex67424)* 25/11/50.
22908 *(ex67436)* 29/8/53.

SHEDS:
  Sheffield 18/5/08.
  Retford 16/2/23.
  Sheffield 28/6/24.

By the second half of the 1930's all forty had eighteen element superheaters and except for odd ones, the standard anti-vacuum valve position was behind the chimney (*see* pages 63, top and 70, top). Neepsend shed.

Numbers 6055 to 6066 had steam operated sanding as original equipment with the sand applied ahead of the leading coupled wheels and behind the rear coupled wheels for either direction of running. Neepsend shed.

The Gorton built engines had gravity sanding and for some years after Grouping still had the metal and rubber shields on the pipe ends to counter wind deflection from the point of application. During the later 1920's all these sand shields were taken off and not replaced. Trafford Park shed.

In the latter years of the LNER the gravity sanding on the Gorton built engines was changed to steam application and not just on the push/pull engines. Guide Bridge.

(above) Equalising pipes between side and bunker water tanks were originally of two types. On the Gorton built engines they were of large square section. On Vulcan built engines they were smaller and circular and many Gorton built engines were later changed.

(left) Ultimately the whole class acquired the circular pipes.

6062 cont./
Wrexham 14/4/27.
Gorton 10/2/28.
Sheffield 17/2/28.
Gorton 14/7/46.
Chester 4/9/46.
Gorton 27/3/47.

RENUMBERED:
6062 24/5/24.
7407 18/4/46.
67407 15/5/48.

CONDEMNED: 10/9/56.
Into Gor. for cut up 22/9/56.

_____

6063

Vulcan 1882.

To traffic 6/1903.

REPAIRS:
Gor. 24/8—26/10/12.**G.**
Gor. 8/7—19/8/16.**G.**
Gor. 19/2—26/3/21.**G.**
Gor. 19/5—25/8/23.**G.**
Gor. 18/7—17/10/25.**G.**
Gor. 15/10—3/12/27.**G.**
Superheated boiler fitted.
Gor. 31/8—12/10/29.**G.**
Gor. 26/12/31—23/1/32.**G.**
Gor. 21/4—5/5/34.**G.**
Gor. 31/12/36—16/1/37.**G.**
Fountain lub. to axles.
Gor. 14/10—11/11/39.**G.**
Gor. 21/7—7/8/43.**G.**
Gor. 29/6—10/8/46.**G.**
Gor. 23—30/8/47.**L.**
Gor. 2—30/10/48.**G.**
Gor. 9—16/4/49.**L.**
Gor. 24/2—10/3/51.**G.**

BOILERS:
  352.
  1256 *(exC14 1126)* 26/10/12.
  362 *(ex193)* 19/8/16.
  732 *(sup.new)* 3/12/27.
  973 *(ex5456)* 23/1/32.
  369 *(new)* 5/5/34.
  743 *(ex5002)* 16/1/37.
  661 *(ex5457)* 11/11/39.
  362 *(ex5190)* 7/8/43.
  739 *(exD6 5853)* 10/8/46.
  4502 *(ex7411)* 30/10/48.
22914 *(ex67436)* 10/3/51.

SHEDS:
Sheffield 2/2/12.
Woodford 14/10/29.
Sheffield 12/11/31.
Barnsley 10/3/32.
Sheffield 23/2/34.
Gorton 12/2/45.

Woodford 13/1/52.
Annesley 25/1/53.
Staveley 19/4/53.

RENUMBERED:
1063c 29/9/23.
6063 17/10/25.
7408 6/10/46.
67408 30/10/48.

CONDEMNED: 10/5/54.
Into Gor. for cut up 15/5/54.

_____

6064

Vulcan 1883.

To traffic 6/1903.

REPAIRS:
Gor. 21/12/12—1/2/13.**G.**
Gor. 25/3—12/8/22.**G.**
Single piece chimney to
Drawing 13685.
Gor. 3/5—19/7/24.**G.**
Gor. 21/1—24/3/28.**G.**
Superheated boiler fitted.
Altered to 13ft gauge.
Gor. 14/9—19/10/29.**G.**
Gor. 1—29/8/31.**G.**
Gor. 13/5—3/6/33.**G.**
Gor. 28/9—12/10/35.**G.**
Gor. 5—26/3/38.**G.**
Gor. 19/10—2/11/40.**G.**
Gor. 16/3—3/4/43.**G.**
Gor. 17/11—15/12/45.**G.**
Gor. 2—30/4/49.**G.**
Gor. 17/2/51.**C/L.**
Gor. 7—21/4/51.**G.**
Gor. 19/9—3/10/53.**G.**

BOILERS:
  353.
  344 *(ex1055)* 1/2/13.
  1016 *(ex454)* 12/8/22.
  733 *(sup.new)* 24/3/28.
  206 *(exD6 5876)* 29/8/31.
  740 *(ex5457)* 3/6/33.
  689 *(exC14 6130)* 12/10/35.
  741 *(ex6062)* 2/11/40.
  4502 *(ex5453)* 3/4/43.
  4513 *(ex7429)* 30/4/49.
  4513 reno. 22913 17/2/51.
22918 *(new)* 21/4/51.
22912 *(ex67418)* 3/10/53.

SHEDS:
Mexborough 27/10/22.
Doncaster 13/12/24.
Sheffield 24/2/26.
Barnsley 25/10/35.
Sheffield 3/2/37.
Barnsley 23/2/37.

Sheffield 21/7/37.
Barnsley 2/10/39.
Colwick 14/3/40.
Trafford Park 22/7/42.
Barnsley 4/1/44.

RENUMBERED:
6064 19/7/24.
7409 10/11/46.
67409 30/4/49.

CONDEMNED: 4/12/56.
Into Gor. for cut up 8/12/56.

_____

6065

Vulcan 1884.

To traffic 6/1903.

REPAIRS:
Gor. 9/12/11—27/1/12.**G.**
Gor. 25/12/20—25/6/21.**G.**
Gor. 21/7—15/9/23.**G.**
Gor. 28/11/25—30/1/26.**G.**
Gor. 5/5—30/6/28.**G.**
Gor. 29/11/30—10/1/31.**G.**
Gor. 18/2—4/3/33.**G.**
Superheated boiler fitted.
Altered to 13ft gauge.
Gor. 24/8—28/9/35.**G.**
Fountain lub. to axles.
Gor. 7—28/5/38.**G.**
Gor. 9—23/12/39.**G.**
Gor. 9/4—2/5/42.**G.**
Gor. 8/7—5/8/44.**G.**
Gor. 25/8—22/9/45.**L.**
After collision.
Gor. 20/4—25/5/46.**G.**
Gor. 17—31/1/48.**L.**
Gor. 19/6—24/7/48.**G.**
Gor. 26/8—16/9/50.**G.**

BOILERS:
  354.
  357 *(ex178)* 27/1/12.
  1257 *(exC14 1126)* 25/6/21.
  739 *(sup.ex5454)* 4/3/33.
  690 *(ex5457)* 28/9/35.
  755 *(exC14 6131)* 28/5/38.
  4511 *(ex5178)* 23/12/39.
  285 *(ex spare)* 2/5/42.
  691 *(exC14 6121)* 5/8/44.
  332 *(ex5002)* 25/5/46.
  358 *(ex7406)* 24/7/48.
22900 *(ex7406)* 16/9/50.

SHEDS:
Sheffield 10/8/08.
Staveley 1/12/28.
Sheffield 3/11/30.
Staveley 16/2/31.
Annesley 16/5/39.
Colwick 28/1/40.

Annesley 4/9/40.
Colwick 30/7/42.
Gorton 6/8/42.
Chester 5/9/44.
Gorton 3/3/46.
Staveley 9/12/51.

RENUMBERED:
1065c 6/10/23.
6065 30/1/26.
7410 25/5/46.
E7410 31/1/48.
67410 24/7/48.

CONDEMNED: 23/3/53.
Into Gor. for cut up 28/3/53.
To Don. for cut up 7/4/53.

_____

6066

Vulcan 1885.

To traffic 6/1903.

REPAIRS:
Gor. 2—16/7/10.**G.**
Gor. 9/5—11/7/14.**G.**
Gor. 2—23/4/21.**G.**
Gor. 4/8—29/9/23.**G.**
Gor. 27/2—19/6/26.**G.**
Gor. 17/3—19/5/28.**G.**
Superheated boiler fitted.
Altered to 13ft gauge.
Gor. 1/2—8/3/30.**G.**
Gor. 30/1—20/2/32.**G.**
Gor. 21/10—11/11/33.**G.**
Gor. 11/4—2/5/36.**G.**
Fountain lub. to axles.
Gor. 13/8—3/9/38.**G.**
Gor. 24/2—21/3/42.**G.**
Gor. 8/12/45—5/1/46.**G.**
Gor. 1—22/5/48.**G.**
Gor. 16/6—28/7/51.**H/I.**
Gor. 22/11—13/12/52.**C/L.**
Gor. 11—25/4/53.**G.**

BOILERS:
  355.
  1014 *(ex55)* 16/7/10.
  349 *(ex1060)* 11/7/14.
  741 *(sup.new)* 19/5/28.
  732 *(ex6063)* 20/2/32.
  967 *(ex5359)* 11/11/33.
  279 *(exD6 5879)* 2/5/36.
  372 *(ex6058)* 3/9/38.
  4507 *(ex5050)* 21/3/42.
  4502 *(ex6064)* 5/1/46.
  4507 *(ex7413)* 22/5/48.
  4507 reno. 22927 28/7/51.
22911 *(ex67429)* 25/4/53.

SHEDS:
Sheffield 13/10/03.
Woodford 20/10/26.

6066 cont./
Sheffield 17/5/28.
Barnsley 3/2/37.
Sheffield 23/2/37.
Gorton 4/12/39.
Barnsley 19/8/42.

RENUMBERED:
1066c 20/10/23.
6066 19/6/26.
7411 20/10/46.
67411 22/5/48.

CONDEMNED: 2/5/55.
Into Gor. for cut up 7/5/55.

5171

Gorton.

To traffic 5/1903.

REPAIRS:
Gor. 19/9—7/11/14.**G.**
Gor. 25/6—30/7/21.**G.**
Furness lub. fitted.
Gor. 7/8—7/11/23.**G.**
Gor. 19/12/25—12/6/26.**G.**
Superheated boiler fitted.
Gor. 14/4—26/5/28.**G.**
Gor. 14/12/29—18/1/30.**G.**
Altered to 13ft gauge.
Gor. 24/9—22/10/32.**G.**
WPU gear removed.
Gor. 22/9—6/10/34.**G.**
Gor. 30/5—20/6/36.**G.**
Gor. 18—25/9/37.**L.**
Gor. 2—23/4/38.**G.**
Gor. 23/12/39—6/1/40.**G.**
Gor. 7—28/11/42.**G.**
Gor. 27/9—7/10/44.**G.**
Gor. 12/4—24/5/47.**G.**
Gor. 21/5—18/6/49.**G.**
Gor. 22—19/4/50.**C/L.**
After collision.
Gor. 12/4—3/5/52.**G.**
Gor. 27—27/2/54.**C/L.**

BOILERS:
  356.
  1017 *(ex455)* 7/11/14.
  686 *(sup.new)* 12/6/26.
  662 *(ex6055)* 22/10/32.
  372 *(new)* 6/10/34.
  733 *(ex5359)* 20/6/36.
  744 *(ex5018)* 23/4/38.
  755 *(ex6065)* 6/1/40.
  686 *(ex6061)* 28/11/42.
  4511 *(exC14 6120)* 7/10/44.
  971 *(ex7403)* 24/5/47.
  4524 *(new)* 18/6/49.
  22905 *(ex67437)* 3/5/52.

SHEDS:
Wrexham 21/10/21.
Bidston 28/6/28.
Wrexham 26/6/29.
Trafford Park 27/3/30.
Wrexham 24/4/30.
Trafford Park 22/12/33.
Northwich 9/10/36.
Gorton 25/11/39.
Ardsley 26/10/41.
Bradford 31/10/41.
Gorton 13/12/41.
Trafford Park 17/1/43.
Chester 29/8/43.
Gorton 5/9/44.
Wrexham 1/7/45.
Gorton 12/8/45.
Northwich 5/5/46.
Gorton 11/8/46.
Wrexham 28/12/52.

RENUMBERED:
  171c 1/12/23.
  5171 12/6/26.
  7412 17/3/46.
  67412 18/6/49.

CONDEMNED: 31/5/54.
Into Don. for cut up 2/7/54.

5178

Gorton.

To traffic 5/1903.

REPAIRS:
Gor. 4/11—16/12/11.**G.**
Gor. 24/3—24/11/17.**G.**
Gor. 1/7—21/10/22.**G.**
Gor. 29/11/24—31/1/25.**G.**
Gor. 30/7—24/9/27.**G.**
Gor. 9/11—21/12/29.**G.**
Superheated boiler fitted.
Altered to 13ft gauge.
Gor. 23/4—14/5/32.**G.**
Gor. 7—21/4/34.**G.**
Gor. 15—29/2/36.**G.**
Gor. 6—13/2/37.**L.**
After collision.
Gor. 6—27/11/37.**G.**
Gor. 14—28/10/39.**G.**
Gor. 22/6—13/7/40.**L.**
Gor. 12/1—7/2/42.**G.**
Gor. 14/1—12/2/44.**G.**
Gor. 8/7/44.**L.**
Gor. 14/1—2/2/46.**G.**
Gor. 28/9—12/10/46.**L.**
Gor. 21/2—20/3/48.**G.**
Gor. 21/5—18/6/49.**G.**
Gor. 21/4—12/5/51.**G.**
Gor. 1/11—22/11/52.**G.**
Gor. 2—23/10/54.**C/L.**

BOILERS:
  357.
  1020 *(ex359)* 16/12/11.
  1006 *(ex9)* 24/11/17.
  978 *(sup.new)* 21/12/29.
  350 *(ex6058)* 21/4/34.
  1595 *(ex5179)* 29/2/36.
  4511 *(new)* 27/11/37.
  368 *(exC14 6122)* 28/10/39.
  350 *(ex5457)* 7/2/42.
  979 *(ex6055)* 12/2/44.
  4507 *(ex6066)* 2/2/46.
  688 *(ex7414)* 20/3/48.
  4523 *(new)* 18/6/49.
  22920 *(ex67408)* 12/5/51.
  22955 *(exC14 67440)* 22/11/52.

SHEDS:
Wrexham 6/1/22.
Heaton Mersey 3/2/25.
Wrexham 28/6/28.
Bidston 9/6/31.
Wrexham 23/5/32.
Trafford Park 7/12/33.
Northwich 9/3/36.
Gorton 31/12/36.
Northwich 25/11/39.
Gorton 2/12/39.
Ardsley 26/10/41.
Bradford 31/10/41.
Gorton 3/1/42.
Chester 21/7/44.

RENUMBERED:
  5178 31/1/25.
  7413 14/7/46.
  67413 20/3/48.

CONDEMNED: 2/12/57.
Into Gor. for cut up 7/12/57.

5179

Gorton.

To traffic 6/1903.

REPAIRS:
Gor. 13/6—8/8/08.**G.**
Gor. 29/7—4/11/16.**G.**
Gor. 14/1—25/3/22.**G.**
Gor. 24/5—9/8/24.**G.**
Gor. 2/10—18/12/26.**G.**
Gor. 20/4—25/5/29.**G.**
Superheated boiler fitted.
Altered to 13ft gauge.
Gor. 13—27/2/32.**G.**
Gor. 16—21/12/35.**G.**
Fountain lub. to axles.
Gor. 12—26/3/38.**G.**
Gor. 27/1—17/2/40.**G.**
Gor. 15/11—13/12/41.**G.**
Gor. 19/4—13/5/44.**G.**

Gor. 6/7—10/8/46.**G.**
Gor. 10/1—7/2/48.**G.**
Gor. 6/8—3/9/49.**G.**
Gor. 4—25/8/51.**G.**
Gor. 3—31/1/53.**L/I.**

BOILERS:
  358.
  1287 *(new)* 8/8/08.
  1256 *(ex1063)* 4/11/16.
  904 *(sup.exD6 5852)* 25/5/29.
  741 *(ex6066)* 27/2/32.
  1595 *(ex5055)* 6/1/34.
  332 *(ex6062)* 21/12/35.
  348 *(ex6055)* 26/3/38.
  4512 *(exD6 5855)* 17/2/40.
  288 *(ex5357)* 13/5/44.
  688 *(ex6055)* 10/8/46.
  4511 *(ex spare)* 7/2/48.
  976 *(ex7427)* 3/9/49.
  22928 *(exC14 67449)* 25/8/51.

SHEDS:
Trafford Park 6/18.
Wrexham 23/4/30.
Bidston 23/1/31.
Wrexham 9/6/31.
Trafford Park 6/1/34.
Gorton 30/11/36.
Trafford Park 24/10/38.
Gorton 11/10/41.
Wrexham 4/2/45.
Gorton 22/9/46.
Chester 5/12/46.
Wrexham 12/6/54.

RENUMBERED:
  5179 9/8/24.
  7414 21/9/46.
  ᴇ**7414** 7/2/48.
  67414 5/3/49.

CONDEMNED: 6/6/55.
Into Gor. for cut up 11/6/55.

5188

Gorton.

To traffic 7/1903.

REPAIRS:
Gor. 4/7—10/10/14.**G.**
Wrx. 7/1—12/7/22.**G.**
Gor. 23/12/22—27/1/23.**G.**
Gor. 16/6—11/8/23.**L.**
Gor. 29/11/24—16/5/25.**G.**
Gor. 28/5—9/7/27.**G.**
Gor. 14/9—26/10/29.**G.**
Superheated boiler fitted.
Altered to 13ft gauge.
Gor. 3—31/10/31.**G.**
Over 13ft gauge.

Engine with single top lamp iron and square pipe for water levelling tanks. Neepsend shed.

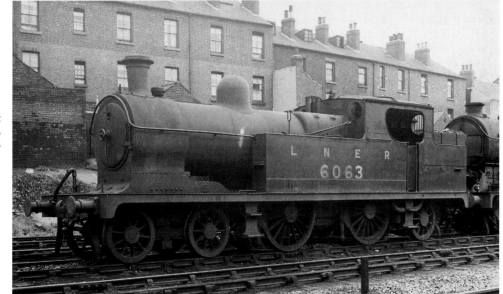

The same engine in almost identical place but now with two top lamp irons and circular levelling pipe. Neepsend shed.

The original chimney was the Robinson design which tapered inwards to the top and which was 13ft 1½in. high from rail level. Two of the class were fitted with a single piece chimney in August 1922 - No.1064 (12th) and No.20 (19th), and this experiment was also extended to Class C14 No.1120 (23rd December 1922) - *see* page 50, middle.

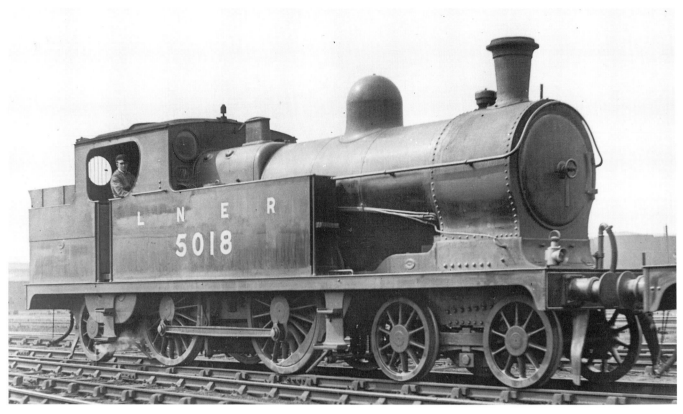

To bring the class within the 13ft 0in. composite loading gauge, from February 1926 a built-up 'plant pot' chimney and a reduced height dome were fitted.

As this class never worked where restriction to 13ft 0in. was of any importance, Gorton were not very punctilious in taking every opportunity of changing engines to it. So there were anomalies of various dome and chimney pairings. This 1926 superheated engine has the shorter dome but until January 1930 kept the original tall chimney. By May 1937 however, all had the 'plant pot' chimney and shorter dome, and all of them remained that way.

(above) **Until after 1934 there were no alterations to the original two open coal rails on the bunker. Wrexham, April 1939.**

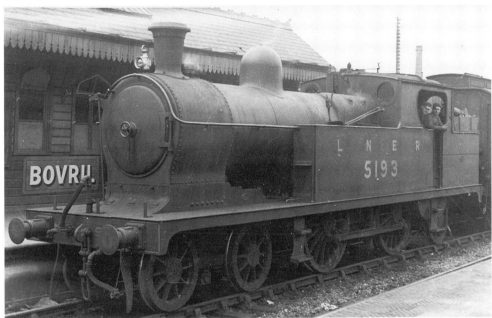

(right) **All then had the rails replaced by plating on the inside of the vertical supports which had been used for the rails.**

In the 1950's at least two of the engines shedded at Gorton had much deeper plating added; No.67417 on 26th April 1952 whilst No.67421 had been so dealt with on 8th December 1951.

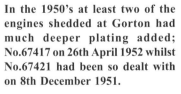

In August/September 1933 six of the class, Nos.5009, 5190, 5191, 5193, 5359, and 5456 were fitted with mechanically operated push-and-pull gear for auto-train working. Dukinfield works.

There was equipment added on both sides of these six engines which were at Wrexham and Bidston sheds for the Seacombe-Wrexham service. Gorton shed.

5188 cont./

5188 cont./
Gor. 17/2—17/3/34.**G.**
Altered to 13ft gauge.
Gor. 21/3—4/4/36 .**G.**
Fountain lub. to axles.
Gor. 21/8—4/9/37.**G.**
Gor. 16—30/9/39.**G.**
Gor. 17/8—5/9/42.**G.**
Gor. 20/5—10/6/44.**G.**
Gor. 19/1—2/2/46.**L.**
Gor. 19/10—9/11/46.**G.**
Gor. 16/10—6/11/48.**G.**
Gor. 5—19/5/51.**G.**
Gor. 26/4—3/5/52.**C/L.**
Gor. 12/9—3/10/53.**G.**

BOILERS:
　359.
　1253 *(exC14 1123)* 10/10/14.
　1723 *(sup.exD6 5854)* 26/10/29.
　297 *(exD6 5857)* 31/10/31.
　663 *(ex5455)* 17/3/34.
　358 *(ex5018)* 4/4/36.
　350 *(ex5191)* 4/9/37.
　358 *(ex5199)* 30/9/39.
　729 *(ex5009)* 5/9/42.
　746 *(ex5455)* 10/6/44.
　4515 *(new)* 9/11/46.
　359 *(exC14 7445)* 6/11/48.
22922 *(ex67435)* 19/5/51.
22903 *(ex67419)* 3/10/53.

SHEDS:
Wrexham 5/12/14.
Heaton Mersey *after* 17/9/26.
Gorton 27/12/27.
Wrexham 7/2/28.
Trafford Park 29/9/31.
Northwich 19/9/34.
Trafford Park 4/4/36.
Gorton 14/12/44.

RENUMBERED:
5188 16/5/25.
7415 5/5/46.
67415 6/11/48.

CONDEMNED: 27/2/56.
Into Gor. for cut up 3/3/56.

5190

Gorton.

To traffic 8/1903.

REPAIRS:
Gor. 15/11—20/12/19.**G.**
Gor. 6/5—1/7/22.**G.**
Gor. 6/12/24—21/2/25.**G.**

Wrx. 4/1—14/3/27.**G.**
Gor. 9/2—20/4/29.**G.**
Superheated boiler fitted.
Altered to 13ft gauge.
Gor. 3—24/10/31.**G.**
Gor. 5—26/8/33.**G.**
Fitted with P&P double end control. WPU gear removed.
Over 13ft gauge.
Gor. 12/1—2/2/35.**G.**
Altered to 13ft gauge.
Fountain lub. to axles.
Gor. 31/12/36— 30/1/37.**G.**
Vacuum P&P gear fitted.
Gor. 25/6—6/8/38.**G.**
Gor. 6—27/4/40.**G.**
Gor. 22/3—10/5/41.**G.**
Gor. 17/6—3/7/43.**G.**
Gor. 7—28/9/46.**G.**
Gor. 31/1—21/2/48.**G.**
Gor. 8/5/48.**L.**
Gor. 25/2—22/4/50.**G.**
Gor. 26/7—23/8/52.**G.**
Gor. 26/6—31/7/54.**G.**
Modified blow-off cock with silencer.
Str. 16—18/8/55.**N/C.**
Additional boiler wash-out plug fitted.
Gor. 11/8—15/9/56.**G.**

BOILERS:
　360.
　1019 *(ex spare)* 20/12/19.
　967 *(sup.new)* 20/4/29.
　733 *(ex6064)* 24/10/31.
　1824 *(exD6 5269)* 26/8/33.
　4503 *(new)* 2/2/35.
　288 *(exD6 5864)* 30/1/37.
　362 *(new)* 27/4/40.
　662 *(ex5029)* 3/7/43.
　4514 *(exD6 5874)* 28/9/46.
22902 *(ex67424)* 23/8/52.
22944 *(ex67433)* 31/7/54.
22923 *(ex spare)* 15/9/56.

SHEDS:
Wrexham 6/1/22.
Gorton 11/9/39.
Bidston 16/10/39.
Gorton 15/3/42.
King's Cross 13/11/50.
Neasden 18/3/51.

RENUMBERED:
5190 21/2/25.
7416 28/9/46.
ᴇ**7416** 21/2/48.
67416 8/5/48.

CONDEMNED: 23/12/58.
Into Gor. for cut up 27/12/58.

5191

Gorton.

To traffic 8/1903.

REPAIRS:
Gor. 19/3—30/4/21.**G.**
Gor. 10/5—19/7/24.**G.**
Gor. 28/8—11/12/26.**G.**
Superheated boiler fitted.
Altered to 13ft gauge.
Gor. 1/9—20/10/28.**G.**
Gor. 1/8—5/9/31.**G.**
Gor. 26/8—16/9/33.**G.**
Fitted with P&P double end control.
WPU gear removed.
Gor. 22/2—14/3/36.**G.**
Fountain lub. to axles.
Gor. 7—28/8/37.**G.**
Vacuum P&P gear fitted.
Gor. 13/5—10/6/39.**G.**
Gor. 25/1—22/2/41.**G.**
Gor. 26/4—10/5/41.**G.**
Damaged by enemy action at Bidston.
Gor. 6—25/9/43.**G.**
Gor. 8/6—6/7/46.**G.**
Gor. 3/4—1/5/48.**G.**
Gor. 12/11—31/12/49.**G.**
Gor. 20/1—3/2/51.**C/L.**
Gor. 5—26/4/52.**G.**
Gor. 21/2/53.**C/L.**
After collision.
Gor. 15/5—19/6/54.**H/I.**
Gor. 2—23/4/55.**C/H.**
Gor. 18/5—8/6/57.**G.**
Gor. 9/1/60 *Not repaired*

BOILERS:
　361.
　694 *(sup.new)* 11/12/26.
　348 *(ex5009)* 16/9/33.
　350 *(ex5178)* 14/3/36.
　4507 *(exC14 6130)* 28/8/37.
　4501 *(ex5029)* 10/6/39.
　739 *(ex5456)* 22/2/41.
　967 *(ex6062)* 25/9/43.
　744 *(exC14 6131)* 6/7/46.
　4517 *(new)* 1/5/48.
　285 *(exC14 7440)* 31/12/49.
　285 *reno. 22909* 3/2/51.
22943 *(ex67431)* 26/4/52.
22939 *(ex67426)* 23/4/55.
22944 *(ex67416)* 8/6/57.

SHEDS:
Trafford Park 6/18.
Wrexham 22/12/33.
Gorton 9/7/42.

RENUMBERED:
5191 19/7/24.
7417 27/4/46.
67417 1/5/48.

CONDEMNED: 20/1/60.
Cut up at Gorton.

5193

Gorton.

To traffic 9/1903.

REPAIRS:
Gor. 24/4—26/6/15.**G.**
Gor. 18/3—17/6/22.**G.**
Gor. 11/10—29/11/24.**G.**
Gor. 18/12/26—12/3/27.**G.**
Gor. 6/7—3/8/29.**G.**
Gor. 11/4—16/5/31.**G.**
Superheated boiler fitted.
Altered to 13ft gaugr.
Gor. 5—26/8/33.**G.**
Fitted with P&P double end control.
WPU gear removed.
Gor. 12—26/10/35.**G.**
Gor. 12/6—3/7/37.**G.**
Vacuum P&P gear fitted.
Gor. 20/8—17/9/38.**G.**
Gor. 26/4—17/5/41.**G.**
Gor. 31/3—17/4/43.**G.**
Gor. 7/7—11/8/45.**G.**
Gor. 15/3—12/4/47.**G.**
Gor. 9/4—14/5/49.**G.**
Gor. 10/2—3/3/51.**G.**
Gor. 2—16/2/52.**C/L.**
After collision.
Gor. 22/11—13/12/52.**G.**
Gor. 11/12/54—22/1/55.**G.**
Modified blow-off cock with silencer.
Str. 29—31/8/55.**N/C.**
Additional boiler wash-out plug fitted.
Gor. 23/11—21/12/57.**G.**
Gor. 27/12/58. *Not repaired.*

BOILERS:
　362.
　351 *(ex1062)* 26/6/15.
　332 *(sup.new)* 16/5/31.
　691 *(exD6 5881)* 26/8/33.
　739 *(ex6065)* 26/10/35.

WORKS CODES:- Cw - Cowlairs. Dar- Darlington. Don - Doncaster. Ghd - Gateshead. Gor - Gorton. Inv - Inverurie. Nor - Norwich. Str - Stratford.
REPAIR CODES:- **C/H** - Casual Heavy. **C/L** - Casual Light. **G** - General. **H**- Heavy. **H/I** - Heavy Intermediate. **L** - Light. **L/I** - Light Intermediate. **N/C** - Non-Classified.

57

5193 cont./
976 (exC14 6120) 17/9/38.
4506 (exD6 5270) 17/4/43.
4501 (ex6060) 11/8/45.
729 (ex7401) 12/4/47.
4515 (ex7415) 14/5/49.
22912 (ex67407) 3/3/51.
22916 (ex67434) 13/12/52.
22962 (new) 22/1/55.
22918 (exC14 67445) 21/12/57.

SHEDS:
Chester 29/4/11.
Wrexham 16/9/33.
Bidston 11/12/33.
Gorton 22/9/38.
Wigan. 3/11/40.
Neasden 18/2/41.
Gorton 18/3/41.
Neasden 2/1/42.

RENUMBERED:
5193 29/11/24.
7418 18/8/46.
67418 14/5/49.

CONDEMNED: 27/12/58.
Cut up at Gorton.

5199

Gorton.

To traffic 9/1903.

REPAIRS:
Gor. 23/9—9/12/16.**G.**
Gor. 22/1—7/5/21.**G.**
Gor. 4/11/22—27/1/23.**G.**
Gor. 28/11/25—13/2/26.**G.**
Gor. 14/7—25/8/28.**G.**
Gor. 30/8—25/10/30.**G.**
Superheated boiler fitted.
Altered to 13ft gauge.
Gor. 31/12/32—28/1/33.**G.**
Gor. 13/7—10/8/35.**G.**
Fountain lub. to axles.
Gor. 6—27/11/37.**G.**
Gor. 26/8—16/9/39.**G.**
Gor. 25/8—25/10/41.**G.**
Gor. 21/5—5/6/43.**G.**
Gor. 22/4—6/5/44.**L.**
Gor. 31/3—21/4/45.**L.**
Gor. 6/7—10/8/46.**G.**
Gor. 9—30/10/48.**G.**
Gor. 7—28/10/50.**G.**
Gor. 15/8—12/9/53.**G.**

BOILERS:
363.
1259 (ex spare) 9/12/16.
357 (ex1065) 7/5/21.
699 (sup.exD6 5866) 25/10/30.
288 (ex5002) 28/1/33.

298 (exC14 6121) 10/8/35.
358 (ex5188) 27/11/37.
285 (ex6061) 16/9/39.
359 (ex5359) 25/10/41.
740 (ex6056) 5/6/43.
967 (ex7417) 10/8/46.
4504 (ex7404) 30/10/48.
22903 (exC14 67450) 28/10/50.
22935 (exC14 67450) 12/9/53.

SHEDS:
Mexborough 20/1/22.
Trafford Park 23/3/23.
Walton-on-the-Hill 4/10/24.
Trafford Park 20 12/24.
Wrexham 30/9/31.
Northwich 27/6/32.
Trafford Park 5/7/33.
Bidston 22/3/42.
Gorton 9/5/43.
Staveley 9/12/51.
Gorton 28/10/56.

RENUMBERED:
5199 13/2/26.
7419 28/4/46.
67419 30/10/48.

CONDEMNED: 10/6/57.
Into Gor. for cut up 15/6/57.

5002

Gorton.

To traffic 8/1904.

REPAIRS:
Gor. 13/11—25/12/15.**G.**
Wrx. 13/7—29/8/21.**G.**
Gor. 21/4—14/7/23.**G.**
Gor. 30/5—1/8/25.**G.**
Gor. 19/11/27—28/1/28.**G.**
Gor. 5/4—10/5/30.**G.**
Superheated boiler fitted.
Altered to 13ft gauge.
Gor. 12—26/11/32.**G.**
Gor. 6—27/10/34.**G.**
Gor. 7—28/11/36.**G.**
Fountain lub. to axles.
Gor. 4—25/2/39.**G.**
Gor. 2—19/7/41.**G.**
Push pull gear fitted.
Gor. 23/10—6/11/43.**G.**
Gor. 3—11/12/43.**L.**
After collision.
Gor. 12—16/9/44.**L.**
Gor. 23/2—23/3/46.**G.**
Gor. 25/10—15/11/47.**G.**
Gor. 7—21/5/49.**G.**
Gor. 9—30/6/51.**G.**
Gor. 27/9—18/10/52.**G.**
Gor. 4/9—9/10/54.G.
Mod.blow-off cock with silencer.

Gor. 14—28/5/55.C/L.
After colision. Add'l. washout plug fitted.
Gor. 16/3—13/4/57.G.
Gor. 13/12/58. *Not repaired.*

BOILERS:
1005.
347 (ex310) 25/12/15.
288 (sup.new) 10/5/30.
743 (exC14 6127) 26/11/32.
972 (ex5047) 28/11/36.
663 (ex5047) 25/2/39.
365 (ex5020) 19/7/41.
731 (exD6 5859) 23/3/46.
329 (ex7405) 15/11/47.
697 (ex7409) 21/5/49.
22926 (ex67413) 30/6/51.
22954 (ex67416) 18/10/52.
22930 (exC14 67446) 9/10/54.
22932 (exC14 67445) 13/4/57.

SHEDS:
Chester.
Northwich 21/5/30.
Gorton 10/11/34.
Chester 28/11/36.
Wigan 30/3/40.
Gorton 15/5/40.
Neasden 6/8/41.

RENUMBERED:
5002 1/8/25.
7420 23/3/46.
67420 21/5/49.

CONDEMNED: 13/12/58.
Cut up at Gorton.

5009

Gorton.

To traffic 9/1904.

REPAIRS:
Gor. 21/10—9/12/16.**G.**
Gor. 4/11/22—13/1/23.**G.**
Gor. 28/11/25—30/1/26.**G.**
Gor. 19/5—28/7/28.**G.**
Gor. 4/7—1/8/31.**G.**
Superheated boiler fitted.
Altered to 13ft gauge.
Gor. 29/7—19/8/33.**G.**
Fitted with P&P double end control.
WPU gear off.
Gor. 13—27/7/35.**G.**
Fountain lub. to axles.
Gor. 13—27/3/36.**G.**
Gor. 25/2—11/3/37.**G.**
Vacuum P&P gear fitted.
Gor. 25/2—11/3/39.**G.**
Gor. 14—28/9/40.**G.**

Gor. 28/7—22/8/42.**G.**
Gor. 14/10—4/11/44.**G.**
Gor. 8/3—12/4/47.**G.**
Gor. 20/8—17/9/49.**G.**
Gor. 6/10—8/12/51.**G.**
Gor. 23/5—20/6/53.**G.**
Gor. 31/3—28/4/56.**G.**

BOILERS:
1006.
1254 (exC14 1120) 9/12/16.
348 (sup.new) 1/8/31.
738 (exC14 6124) 19/8/33.
4509 (new) 27/7/35.
327 (exC14 6129) 27/3/37.
972 (ex5002) 11/3/39.
729 (exC14 6125) 28/9/40.
348 (ex5028) 22/8/42.
686 (ex5171) 4/11/44.
975 (ex7436) 12/4/47.
978 (exC14 7449) 17/9/49.
22934 (exC14 67445) 8/12/51.
22907 (exC14 67447) 20/6/53.
22947 (exC14 67442) 28/4/56.

SHEDS:
Chester 26/11/09.
Heaton Mersey 23/3/23.
Chester *by* 17/9/26.
Northwich 2/6/30.
Trafford Park 31/8/31.
Wrexham 25/9/33.
Gorton 8/7/42.

RENUMBERED:
5009 30/1/26.
7421 26/5/46.
67421 17/9/49.

CONDEMNED: 5/12/58.
Into Gor. for cut up 6/12/58.

5018

Gorton.

To traffic 9/1904.

REPAIRS:
Gor. 1/5—24/7/15.**G.**
Superheated boiler fitted.
Gor. 19/8—14/4/23.**G.**
Gor. 15/8—24/10/25.**G.**
Gor. 17/3—5/5/28.**G.**
Gor. 18/10—15/11/30.**G.**
Gor. 25/2—11/3/33.**G.**
Altered to 13ft gauge.
Gor. 21/4—12/5/34.**G.**
Gor. 7—21/3/36.**G.**
Fountain lub. to axles.
Gor. 12/3—2/4/38.**G.**
Gor. 15/6—6/7/40.**G.**
Gor. 26/3—11/4/42.**G.**
Gor. 6/11—4/12/43.**G.**

In 1936/1937 mechanical operation was changed to vacuum controlled type, the rods on the right hand side being removed. Two more engines had vacuum controlled type fitted, Nos.5002 and 5115, both ex works on 19th July 1941 for working from Neasden shed on the Chalfont-Chesham branch. Gorton works.

Sight feed lubrication from the cab was standard even after superheating and No.5018 was changed to this type (*see* page 54, top) from the Wakefield mechanical put on in 1915.

In 1946 Wakefield mechanical lubricators were put on the engines fitted for push-and-pull working. Nos.7416, 7417, 7418, 7420, 7421, 7433 and 7436 certainly got it, but if 7438 did so, it was removed by 1955 (*see* below).

No.67438 was the only one of the eight push-and-pull fitted engines noted as being without the Wakefield mechanical lubricator.

5018 cont./
Gor. 3—14/10/44.**L.**
Gor. 10/11—8/12/45.**H.**
Gor. 17/1—7/2/48.**G.**
Gor. 10/6—1/7/50.**G.**
Gor. 21/6—16/8/52.**G.**

BOILERS:
1007.
1563 *(sup.new)* 24/7/15.
1794 *(exD6 5868)* 15/11/30.
358 *(new)* 11/3/33.
744 *(ex5114)* 21/3/36.
660 *(exD6 5871)* 2/4/38.
690 *(ex5028)* 6/7/40.
697 *(exD6 5859)* 4/12/43.
4506 *(ex5193)* 8/12/45.
4518 *(new)* 7/2/48.
349 *(ex67405)* 1/7/50.
22950 *(ex67428)* 16/8/52.

SHEDS:
Trafford Park
Chester 5/5/46.
Gorton 5/12/46.

RENUMBERED:
5018 24/10/25.
7422 19/5/46.
E**7422** 7/2/48.
67422 1/7/50.

CONDEMNED: 27/9/54.
Into Gor. for cut up 2/10/54.

5020

Gorton.

To traffic 10/1904.

REPAIRS:
Gor. 20/10—2/12/11.**G.**
Gor. 13—19/8/22.**G.**
Single piece chimney to Drawing 13685.
Gor. 20/12/24—30/5/25.**G.**
Gor. 22/10—10/12/27.**G.**
Gor. 5/10—16/11/29.**G.**
Gor. 28/5—18/6/32.**G.**
Gor. 25/8—22/9/34.**G.**
Superheated boiler fitted.
Altered to 13ft gauge.
Gor. 29/8—26/9/36.**G.**
Fountain lub. to axles.
Gor. 9/10/37.**L.**
Gor. 7/1—11/2/39.**G.**
Gor. 1—22/7/39.**L.**
After collision.
Gor. 3—31/5/41.**G.**
Gor. 8—19/6/43.**G.**
Gor. 20/10—10/11/45.**G.**
Gor. 1—29/11/47.**G.**
Gor. 21/1—11/2/50.**G.**

Gor. 9—16/9/50.**G.**
Gor. 20/9—11/10/52.**G.**
Gor. 19/3—16/4/55.**G.**

BOILERS:
1008.
76 *(new)* 2/12/11.
359 *(ex1062)* 19/8/22.
1258 *(exC14 6128)* 30/5/25.
521 *(sup.ex6061)* 22/9/34.
365 *(ex6058)* 26/9/36.
353 *(exC14 6130)* 31/5/41.
359 *(ex5199)* 19/6/43.
4503 *(ex5453)* 10/11/45.
690 *(exC14 7448)* 29/11/47.
4517 reno. 22901 16/9/50.
22953 *(ex67422)* 11/10/52.
22916 *(ex67418)* 16/4/55.

SHEDS:
Heaton Mersey 17/11/22.
Trafford Park 25/9/29.
Northwich 15/5/30.
Trafford Park 22/9/34.
Gorton 11/4/41.
Ardsley 26/10/41.
Bradford 31/10/41.
Trafford Park 5/6/42.
Gorton 4/7/43.
Barnsley 16/12/56.

RENUMBERED:
5020 30/5/25.
7423 25/5/46.
67423 18/6/49.

CONDEMNED: 14/10/57.
Into Gor. for cut up 19/10/57.

5027

Gorton.

To traffic 10/1904.

REPAIRS:
Gor. 25/10/13—24/1/14.**G.**
Gor. 4/11/22—17/3/23.**G.**
Gor. 18/4—4/7/25.**G.**
Gor. 7/1—25/2/28.**G.**
Gor. 1—29/3/30.**G.**
Superheated boiler fitted.
Altered to 13ft gauge.
Gor. 15/10—5/11/32.**G.**
WPU gear removed.
Over 13ft gauge.
Gor. 2—16/3/35.**G.**
Fountain lub. to axles.
Gor. 13/2—6/3/37.**G.**
Altered to 13ft gauge.
Gor. 11—25/3/39.**G.**
Gor. 22/2—15/3/41.**G.**
Gor. 20/8—4/9/43.**G.**

Gor. 28—30/10/43.**L.**
Gor. 28/10—4/11/44.**L.**
Gor. 6/4—11/5/46.**G.**
Gor. 11/8—11/9/48.**G.**
Gor. 7—28/10/50.**G.**
Gor. 21/6—5/7/52.**G.**
Gor. 19/2—26/3/55.**G.**
Gor. 22/6—13/7/57.**N/C.**

BOILERS:
1009.
1012 *(ex47)* 24/1/14.
279 *(sup.new)* 29/3/30.
900 *(exD6 5875)* 5/11/32.
1824 *(ex5190)* 16/3/35.
662 *(exC14 6127)* 6/3/37.
327 *(ex5009)* 25/3/39.
521 *(ex5047)* 15/3/41.
693 *(ex5050)* 4/9/43.
660 *(exC14 6124)* 11/5/46.
369 *(exC14 7446)* 11/9/48.
22902 *(ex67410)* 28/10/50.
22948 *(exS.B.635)* 5/7/52.
22942 *(ex67437)* 26/3/55.

SHEDS:
Trafford Park
Northwich 19/7/30.
Trafford Park 25/7/30.
Gorton 11/10/41.
Wrexham 8/3/42.
Trafford Park 28/3/43.
Gorton 5/5/46.
Darnall 22/3/53.

RENUMBERED:
5027 4/7/25.
7424 17/3/46.
67424 11/9/48.

CONDEMNED: 14/11/58.
Into Gor. for cut up 15/11/58..

5028

Gorton.

To traffic 11/1904.

REPAIRS:
Gor. 4/8—2/9/11.**G.**
Gor. 30/5—26/9/14.**G.**
Gor. 30/9/22—20/1/23.**G.**
Gor. 14/3—16/5/25.**G.**
Gor. 30/4—18/6/27.**G.**
Gor. 5/10—16/11/29.**G.**
Gor. 5—26/7/30.**L.**
Gor. 26/3—16/4/32.**G.**
Gor. 4/8—1/9/34.**G.**
Superheated boiler fitted.
Altered to 13ft gauge.
Gor. 25/7—15/8/36.**G.**
Fountain lub. to axles.
Gor. 14/5—4/6/38.**G.**

Gor. 25/5—8/6/40.**G.**
Gor. 16/2—14/3/42.**G.**
Gor. 6—27/5/44.**G.**
Gor. 5—26/10/46.**G.**
Gor. 1—8/5/48.**H.**
Gor. 29/1/49.**L.**
Gor. 30/4—21/5/49.**G.**
Gor. 25/8—22/9/51.**G.**
Gor. 6/3—3/4/54.**G.**

BOILERS:
1010.
358 *(ex179)* ?/?/09.
1014 *(ex1066)* 26/9/14.
226 *(ex6061)* 16/4/32.
975 *(sup.ex5029)* 1/9/34.
349 *(ex6056)* 15/8/36.
690 *(ex6065)* 4/6/38.
348 *(ex5179)* 8/6/40.
368 *(ex5178)* 14/3/42.
4512 *(ex5179)* 27/5/44.
742 *(ex5114)* 26/10/46.
521 *(exC14 7441)* 21/5/49.
22931 *(new)* 22/9/51.
22904 *(ex67407)* 3/4/54.

SHEDS:
Wrexham 9/12/21.
Heaton Mersey *after* 17/9/26.
Trafford Park 25/9/29.
Northwich 16/5/30.
Trafford Park 9/9/32.
Gorton 7/1/42.

RENUMBERED:
5028 16/5/25.
7425 17/3/46.
67425 8/5/48.

CONDEMNED: 6/8/56.
Into Dar. for cut up 25/8/56.

5047

Gorton.

To traffic 11/1904.

REPAIRS:
Gor. 26/7—25/10/13.**G.**
Gor. 15/4—22/7/22.**G.**
Gor. 10/5—6/9/24.**G.**
Gor. 25/9—25/12/26.**G.**
Gor. 1/12/28—19/1/29.**G.**
Gor. 12/12/31—9/1/32.**G.**
Superheated boiler fitted.
Altered to 13ft gauge.
Gor. 28/4—12/5/34.**G.**
Gor. 29/8—26/9/36.**G.**
Fountain lub. to axles.
Gor. 12—26/11/38.**G.**
Gor. 22/7/39.**L.**
Gor. 8/2—1/3/41.**G.**
Gor. 16/2—7/3/42.**L.**

Until November 1946, all had Ramsbottom safety valves, many of them retaining the open type originally fitted.

(above) A number had the valves in a neat rectangular metal casing, but there was no rule as to this fitting.

(left) Beginning in November 1946, new boilers were fitted with Ross 'pop' safety valves but only No.7415 in November 1946 got one of these boilers whilst in LNER livery.

Until during the 1939-1945 war, it was standard to have the upper lamp iron on top of the smokebox, and a wheel and handle for the smokebox door fastening.

During the war, the wheels were replaced by another handle clad the upper lamp iron was moved on to the smokebox door for easier access. Note the anti-vacuum valve still at end of the header following a 28th September 1946 repair.

5047 cont./
After collision.
Gor. 22/9—2/10/43.**G.**
Gor. 14/9—5/10/46.**G.**
Gor. 26/2—26/3/49.**G.**
Gor. 2/2—1/3/52.**G.**
Gor. 13—20/6/53.**C/L.**
Gor. 17—24/4/54.**C/L.**
After collision.

BOILERS:
 1012.
  350 *(ex1061)* 25/10/13.
  754 *(new)* 6/9/24.
  1623 *(sup.exD6 5870)* 9/1/32.
  972 *(exC14 6131)* 12/5/34.
  663 *(ex5188)* 26/9/36.
  521 *(ex6060)* 26/11/38.
  332 *(ex6059)* 1/3/41.
  521 *(ex5027)* 2/10/43.
  362 *(ex6063)* 5/10/46.
  4521 *(new)* 26/3/49.
 22939 *(new)* 1/3/52.

SHEDS:
Chester 27/12/13.
Trafford Park 24/9/36.
Gorton 25/1/42.
Trafford Park 7/10/45.
Gorton 28/10/45.

RENUMBERED:
 5047 6/9/24.
 7426 19/10/46.
 67426 26/3/49.

CONDEMNED: 13/12/54.
Into Don. for cut up 24/12/54.

_____

5029

Gorton.

To traffic 11/1904.

REPAIRS:
Gor. 21/12/12—25/1/13.**G.**
Gor. 15/10—4/2/22.**G.**
Gor. 18/11—16/12/22.**G.**
New cylinders.
Gor. 7/2—11/4/25.**G.**
Gor. 30/5—13/6/25.**L.**
After collision.
Gor. 16/7—3/9/27.**G.**
Gor. 14/9—26/10/29.**G.**
Superheated boiler fitted.
Altered to 13ft gauge.
Gor. 30/1—20/2/32.**G.**
Gor. 30/6—14/7/34.**G.**
WPU gear removed.

Gor. 26/12/36—9/1/37.**G.**
Fountain lub. to axles.
Gor. 29/4—13/5/39.**G.**
Gor. 5—26/4/41.**G.**
Gor. 12—26/6/43.**G.**
Gor. 3—24/3/45.**G.**
Gor. 3/8/46.**L.**
After collision.
Gor. 2—23/8/47.**G.**
Gor. 2/7—6/8/49.**G.**
Gor. 1—22/3/52.**G.**
Gor. 1—22/5/54.**G.**

BOILERS:
 1011.
 1021 *(ex 310)* 25/1/13.
  76 *(ex20)* 4/2/22.
  975 *(sup.new)* 26/10/29.
  661 *(exD6 5880)* 14/7/34.
 4501 *(ex5115)* 9/1/37.
  662 *(ex5027)* 13/5/39.
 4513 *(ex6059)* 26/6/43.
  298 *(exC14 6128)* 24/3/45.
  976 *(ex7402)* 23/8/47.
  971 *(ex7412)* 6/8/49.
 22940 *(ex67426)* 22/3/52.
 22922 *(ex67415)* 22/5/54.

SHEDS:
Trafford Park 16/11/18.
Heaton Mersey 26/1/23.
Trafford Park 25/9/29.
Chester 4/1/30.
Gorton 28/11/36.
Trafford Park 2/4/37.
Wrexham 5/9/43.
Gorton 4/2/45.
Chester 3/3/46.
Gorton 4/9/46.
Langwith Jct. 24/10/54.
Ardsley 15/5/55.

RENUMBERED:
 5029 11/4/25.
 7427 17/3/46.
 67427 6/8/49.

CONDEMNED: 6/1/58.
Into Gor. for cut up 11/1/58.

_____

5050

Gorton.

To traffic 12/1904.
.
REPAIRS:
Gor. 22/6—20/7/12.**G.**
Gor. 29/4—9/12/22.**G.**
Gor. 13/12/24—14/2/25.**G.**

Gor. 28/1—17/3/28.**G.**
Gor. 12/7—16/8/30.**G.**
Gor. 3/9—8/10/32.**G.**
Superheated boiler fitted.
Altered to 13ft gauge.
WPU gear removed.
Gor. 5—26/1/35.**G.**
Fountain lub. to axles.
Gor. 13—27/3/37.**G.**
Gor. 27/5—24/6/39.**G.**
Gor. 19/11—13/12/41.**G.**
Gor. 7—14/8/43.**G.**
Gor. 2—30/6/45.**G.**
Gor. 29/3—10/5/47.**G.**
Gor. 22/5—26/6/48.**G.**
Gor. 19/2/49.**L.**
Fire hole fracture.
Gor. 12/3/49.**C/L.**
Fire hole fracture.
Gor. 18/2—11/3/50.**G.**
Gor. 10—31/5/52.**G.**
Gor. 23/1—13/2/54.**G.**
Gor. 24/12/55—14/1/56.**C/L.**

BOILERS:
 1013.
  354 *(ex1065)* 20/7/12.
  360 *(ex spare)* 9/12/22.
  746 *(sup.exD6 5863)* 8/10/32.
 4502 *(new)* 26/1/35.
 1824 *(ex5027)* 27/3/37.
 4507 *(ex5191)* 24/6/39.
  693 *(exD6 5865)* 13/12/41.
  972 *(ex5456)* 14/8/43.
 4513 *(ex5029)* 30/6/45.
  330 *(ex7431)* 10/5/47.
  744 *(ex7417)* 26/6/48.
 4526 *(new)* 11/3/50.
 22909 *(ex67417)* 31/5/52.
 22961 *(new)* 13/2/54.

SHEDS:
Trafford Park 17/8/18.
Wrexham 7/4/28.
Bidston 26/6/29.
Wrexham 12/7/29.
Trafford Park 30/6/30.
Northwich 31/8/31.
Trafford Park 2/2/35.
Wrexham 13/6/35.
Chester 24/5/38.
Wigan 30/3/40.
Gorton 15/5/40.
Chester 8/3/42.
Wrexham 26/3/44.

RENUMBERED:
 5050 14/2/25.
 7428 19/5/46.
 67428 26/6/48.

CONDEMNED: 29/11/57.
Into Gor. for cut up 30/11/57.

_____

5055

Gorton.

To traffic 12/1904.

REPAIRS:
Gor. 23/10—27/11/09.**G.**
Gor. 6/8/21—7/1/22.**G.**
Gor. 23/6—22/9/23.**G.**
Gor. 1/5—31/7/26.**G.**
Gor. 17/11/28—12/1/29.**G.**
Gor. 23/5—27/6/31.**G.**
Superheated boiler fitted.
Altered to 13ft gauge.
Gor. 2—23/12/33.**G.**
WPU gear removed.
Gor. 4/7—1/8/36.**G.**
Fountain lub. to axles.
Gor. 10—31/12/38.**G.**
Gor. 21/11—27/12/41.**G.**
Gor. 28/12/43—22/1/44.**G.**
Gor. 28/7—1/9/45.**G.**
Gor. 19/4—7/6/47.**G.**
Gor. 12/2—12/3/49.**G.**
Gor. 10—24/2/51.**G.**
Gor. 10/1—7/2/53.**G.**
Gor. 4—18/4/53.**H.**

BOILERS:
 1014.
 1010 *(ex28)* 27/11/09.
 1595 *(sup.exD6 5872)* 27/6/31.
  359 *(new)* 23/12/33.
  746 *(ex5115)* 31/12/38.
 4510 *(exD6 5859)* 27/12/41.
  365 *(ex5002)* 22/1/44.
  361 *(exC14 6123)* 1/9/45.
 4513 *(ex7428)* 7/6/47.
 4508 *(exC14 7447)* 12/3/49.
 22911 *(exC14 67447)* 24/2/51.
 22920 *(ex67413)* 7/2/53.

SHEDS:
Chester.
Northwich 23/10/39.
Wigan 30/3/40.
Gorton 9/5/40.
Wrexham 8/3/42.

RENUMBERED:
 55c 13/10/23.
 5055 31/7/26.
 7429 19/5/46.
 67429 12/3/49.

WORKS CODES:- Cw - Cowlairs. Dar- Darlington. Don - Doncaster. Ghd - Gateshead. Gor - Gorton. Inv - Inverurie. Nor - Norwich. Str - Stratford.
REPAIR CODES:- **C/H** - Casual Heavy. **C/L** - Casual Light. **G** - General. **H** - Heavy. **H/I** - Heavy Intermediate. **L** - Light. **L/I** - Light Intermediate. **N/C** - Non-Classified.

64

At Grouping, all were in GCR lined green livery with a large brass numberplate and also the number was in shaded transfers on the back of the bunker.

During March/April 1923, Gorton continued with the GCR painting style but with 7½in. L.&N.E.R. lettering and 12in. numbers applied by transfers on the tanks. When No.18 was ex paint shop on 26th May 1923 it was in black with single red lining (*see* page 44, bottom).

From September 1923 to the end of January 1924, the area suffix C was added to the number, but GCR style numberplates continued to be fitted. Those to get the suffix were: 1060 (18th September), 1063 (29th September), 1065 (6th October), 55 (13th October), 1066 (20th October), 171 (1st December), 1058 (8th December) and 114 (5th January 1924). All the dates are ex paint shop.

Beginning with No.6055 on 9th February 1924, a 5000 addition was made to the number and the C suffix was discarded. By August 1924 small LNER plates had supplanted the large brass GCR type on the bunker.

Black painting with single red lining continued in use until November 1942 when the lining was no longer applied.

5055 cont./
CONDEMNED: 13/12/54.
Into Don. for cut up 23/12/54.

___

5457

Gorton.

To traffic 1/1905.

REPAIRS:
Gor. 28/8/15—15/1/16.**G.**
Gor. 12/11/21—11/2/22.**G.**
Wrx. 6/12/23—13/2/24.**G.**
Gor. 15/8—17/10/25.**G.**
Gor. 10/3—28/4/28.**G.**
Superheated boiler fitted.
Altered to 13ft gauge.
Gor. 4/4—9/5/31.**G.**
Gor. 1—15/4/33.**G.**
Gor. 10—24/8/35.**G.**
Fountain lub. to axles.
Gor. 1—22/5/37.**G.**
Gor. 30/9—28/10/39.**G.**
Gor. 2/12/41—3/1/42.**G.**
Gor. 18/2—4/3/44.**G.**
Gor. 8/6—6/7/46.**G.**
Gor. 6—27/3/48.**G.**
Gor. 23/4—14/5/49.**G.**
Gor. 25/2—4/3/50.**C/L.**
Gor. 16/6—21/7/51.**G.**
Gor. 26/9—10/10/53.**G.**

BOILERS:
1015.
1250 *(exC14 1129)* 15/1/16.
 740 *(sup.new)* 28/4/28.
 690 *(exD6 5874)* 15/4/33.
 738 *(ex5009)* 24/8/35.
 661 *(ex5029)* 22/5/37.
 350 *(ex5188)* 28/10/39.
 742 *(exD6 5879)* 3/1/42.
4510 *(ex5055)* 4/3/44.
 372 *(ex5310)* 6/7/46.
4506 *(ex7422)* 27/3/48.
22925 *(new)* 21/7/51.
22924 *(exC14 67449)* 10/10/53.

SHEDS:
Chester.
Wrexham 21/5/33.
Chester 18/10/33.
Wrexham 21/9/34.
Trafford Park 13/6/35.
Northwich 26/12/35.
Gorton 15/2/37.
Northwich 1/11/39.
Wigan 30/3/40.
Gorton 17/4/40.
Chester 5/1/47.
Wrexham 20/1/48.

RENUMBERED:
5457 13/2/24.
7430 6/7/46.
67430 27/3/48.

CONDEMNED: 23/4/56.
Into Gor. for cut up 28/4/56.

___

5454

Gorton.

To traffic 2/1905.

REPAIRS:
Gor. 10/12/21—4/3/22.**G.**
Gor. 17/5—19/7/24.**G.**
Wrx. 6/3—3/6/26.**H.**
Gor. 3/3—28/4/28.**G.**
Superheated boiler fitted.
Altered to 13ft gauge.
Gor. 31/5—5/7/30.**G.**
Gor. 21/1—4/2/33.**G.**
Gor. 5—26/10/35.**G.**
Gor. 27/11—18/12/37.**G.**
Gor. 13—27/1/40.**G.**
Gor. 29/12/42—23/1/43.**G.**
Gor. 12—15/4/44.**L.**
Gor. 13/1—10/2/45.**G.**
Gor. 4—25/1/47.**G.**
Gor. 29/5—19/6/48.**G.**
Gor. 24/9—15/10/49.**G.**
Gor. 1—22/3/52.**G.**
Gor. 16/1—6/2/54.**G.**

BOILERS:
1016.
1021 *(ex29)* 4/3/22.
 739 *(sup.new)* 28/4/28.
 699 *(ex5199)* 4/2/33.
 361 *(exD6 5856)* 26/10/35.
4504 *(ex5359)* 18/12/37.
1595 *(ex6055)* 27/1/40.
 329 *(ex5115)* 23/1/43.
 330 *(ex5115)* 10/2/45.
 368 *(exC14 7441)* 25/1/47.
4525 *(new)* 15/10/49.
22941 *(new)* 22/3/52.
22960 *(new)* 6/2/54.

SHEDS:
Wrexham
Gorton 7/2/28.
Trafford Park 25/5/28.
Gorton 22/10/36.
Northwich 31/12/36.
Gorton 11/9/39.
Wigan 4/8/40.
Gorton 15/8/40.
Wigan 7/2/41.
Gorton 10/4/41.
Bradford 20/9/41.
Gorton 13/2/42.
Northwich 3/3/46.

Gorton 14/7/46.

RENUMBERED:
5454 19/7/24.
7431 28/4/46.
67431 19/6/48.

CONDEMNED: 22/10/56.
Into Gor. for cut up 27/10/56.

___

5455

Gorton.

To traffic 2/1905.

REPAIRS:
Gor. 4/4—25/7/14.**G.**
Wrx. 4/1—14/5/21.**H.**
Wrx. 28/2—6/7/23.**G.**
Gor. 19/12/25—27/2/26.**G.**
Superheated boiler fitted.
Altered to 13ft gauge.
Gor. 21/7—25/8/28.**G.**
Gor. 27/6—25/7/31.**G.**
Gor. 27/1—10/2/34.**G.**
Gor. 29/8—3/10/36.**G.**
Fountain lub. to axles.
Gor. 3/9—8/10/38.**G.**
Gor. 30/3—13/4/40.**G.**
After collision.
Gor. 2—20/6/42.**G.**
Gor. 15/4—9/5/44.**G.**
Gor. 24/2—17/3/45.**L.**
Gor. 13/4—11/5/46.**G.**
Gor. 31/12/47—24/1/48.**G.**
Gor. 24/12/49—21/1/50.**G.**
Gor. 28/10—18/11/50.**C/L.**
Gor. 6/10—15/12/51.**H/I.**
Gor. 28/11—12/12/53.**C/L.**

BOILERS:
1017.
1252 *(exC14 1122)* 25/7/14.
 663 *(sup.new)* 27/2/26.
 757 *(ex6056)* 10/2/34.
 975 *(ex5028)* 3/10/36.
 279 *(ex6066)* 8/10/38.
4503 *(exD6 5865)* 13/4/40.
 746 *(ex5055)* 20/6/42.
 350 *(ex5178)* 9/5/44.
 972 *(ex7439)* 24/1/48.
 741 *(exC14 67444)* 21/1/50.
 741 reno. 22906 18/11/50.

SHEDS:
Wrexham 10/2/19.
Chester *by* 26/10/23.
Wrexham 2/2/32.
Bidston 15/4/32.
Wrexham 4/6/32.
Chester 20/2/33.
Wrexham 1/11/36.
Gorton 10/8/38.

Trafford Park 1/11/38.
Gorton 7/5/42.
Wrexham 30/7/42.

RENUMBERED:
5455 27/2/26.
7432 11/5/46.
E**7432** 24/1/48.
67432 14/5/49.

CONDEMNED: 27/12/54.
Into Gor. for cut up 1/1/55.

___

5456

Gorton.

To traffic 3/1905.

REPAIRS:
Gor. 20/5—24/6/11.**G.**
Gor. 17/4—19/6/20.**G.**
Gor. 25/2—27/5/22.**G.**
Gor. 6/12/24—14/2/25.**G.**
Gor. 1/10—26/11/27.**G.**
Gor. 1/6—20/7/29.**G.**
Superheated boiler fitted.
Altered to 13ft gauge.
Gor. 12/12/31—9/1/32.**G.**
Gor. 16—30/9/33.**G.**
Fitted with P&P double end
control.
WPU gear removed.
Gor. 31/3—28/4/34.**H.**
Gor. 4/4—30/5/36.**G.**
Vacuum P&P gear fitted.
Fountain lub. to axles.
Gor. 8—29/10/38.**G.**
Gor. 2—16/11/40.**G.**
Gor. 6/7—7/8/43.**G.**
Gorton 5—19/8/44.**L.**
Gor. 9—23/2/46.**G.**
Gor. 10/4—1/5/48.**G.**
Gor. 4—18/3/50.**G.**
Gor. 5/4—10/5/52.**G.**
Gor. 13/3—3/4/54.**G.**

BOILERS:
1018.
 536 *(new)* 24/6/11.
1255 *(ex spare)* 19/6/20.
 973 *(sup.new)* 20/7/29.
 161 *(ex6058)* 9/1/32.
 694 *(ex5191)* 30/9/33.
 978 *(ex5178)* 28/4/34.
 739 *(ex5193)* 29/10/38.
 972 *(ex5009)* 16/11/40.
 353 *(ex5020)* 7/8/43.
 979 *(ex5178)* 23/2/46.
 365 *(exD6 5855)* 1/5/48.
4527 *(new)* 18/3/50.
22944 *(new)* 10/5/52.
22925 *(ex67430)* 3/4/54.

SHEDS:
Trafford Park 1/9/22.
Chester 19/12/28.
Wrexham 10/1/29.
Gorton 11/9/39.
Wrexham 19/6/40.
Gorton 2/12/41.
Wrexham 22/9/46.
Northwich 17/10/48.
Chester 30/4/50.
Retford 7/11/55.
Ardsley 27/11/55.
Copley Hill 29/1/56.
Ardsley 10/3/57.

RENUMBERED:
5456 14/2/25.
7433 13/7/46.
67433 1/5/48.

CONDEMNED: 6/1/58.
Into Gor. for cut up 11/1/58.

5310

Gorton.

To traffic 4/1905.

REPAIRS:
Gor. 15/6—20/7/12.**G**.
Gor. 10/7—27/11/15.**G**.
Gor. 26/11/21—25/2/22.**G**.
Gor. 19/7—27/9/24.**G**.
Gor. 11/6—13/8/27.**G**.
Superheated boiler fitted.
Altered to 13ft gauge.
Gor. 18/1—15/2/30.**G**.
Gor. 18/6—16/7/32.**G**.
Gor. 26/8—16/9/33.**G**.
WPU gear removed.
Gor. 30/5—13/6/36.**G**.
Fountain lub. to axles.
Gor. 25/6—16/7/38.**G**.
Gor. 6—20/7/40.**G**.
Gor. 2/8/41.**C/L**.
Gor. 24/3—4/4/42.**G**.
Gor. 4/5—1/6/46.**G**.
Gor. 12/3—9/4/49.**G**.
Gor. 24/2—17/3/51.**C/L**.
After collision.
Gor. 21/6—5/7/52.**G**.
Gor. 19/2—26/3/55.**G**.
Gor. 30/5—10/6/55.**N/C**.

BOILERS:
1021.
347 (ex1058) 20/7/12.
1023 (ex114) 27/11/15.
729 (sup.new) 13/8/27.
697 (ex6056) 16/7/32.
329 (exC14 6130) 16/9/33.
967 (ex6066) 13/6/36.
288 (ex5190) 20/7/40.

372 (ex6066) 4/4/42.
691 (ex6065) 1/6/46.
4510 (exC14 7451) 9/4/49.
4510 reno. 22916 17/3/51.
22949 (ex67438) 5/7/52.
22940 (ex67427) 26/3/55.

SHEDS:
Chester 23/8/13.
Woodford 27/7/32.
Chester 16/9//33.
Gorton 24/5/38.
Bradford 20/9/41.
Barnsley 11/7/42.

RENUMBERED:
5310 27/9/24.
7434 1/6/46.
67434 9/4/49.

CONDEMNED: 3/10/57.
Into Gor. for cut up 5/10/57.

5357

Gorton.

To traffic 4/1905.

REPAIRS
Gor. 16/2—4/5/18.**G**.
Gor. 24/12/21—11/2/22.**G**.
Gor. 6/12/24—14/2/25.**G**.
Gor. 12/3—14/5/27.**G**.
Gor. 11/5—22/6/29.**G**.
Gor. 11/7—8/8/31.**G**.
Superheated boiler fitted.
Altered to 13ft gauge.
Gor. 23/12/33—13/1/34.**G**.
Gor. 23/2—16/3/35.**G**.
Fountain lub. to axles.
Gor. 29/5—19/6/37.**G**.
Gor. 11—25/11/39.**G**.
Gor. 25/5—13/6/42.**G**.
Gor. 17/2—11/3/44.**G**.
Gor. 10—24/11/45.**G**.
Gor. 28/6—9/8/47.**G**.
Gor. 1/11/47.**L**.
Gor. 23/4—21/5/49.**G**.
Gor. 27/5—10/6/50.**C/L**.
Gor. 7—28/4/51.**G**.

BOILERS:
1019.
1020 (ex178) 4/5/18.
349 (sup.new) 8/8/31.
353 (ex5114) 13/1/34.
738 (ex5457) 19/6/37.
743 (ex6063) 25/11/39.
288 (ex5310) 13/6/42.
4504 (ex6057) 11/3/44.
743 (exD6 5855) 24/11/45.
361 (ex7429) 9/8/47.
4522 (new) 21/5/49.

22919 (ex67429) 28/4/51.

SHEDS:
Trafford Park 17/8/18.
Wrexham 10/12/28.
Bidston 12/7/29.
Wrexham 23/1/30.
Trafford Park 23/4/30.
Gorton 22/2/37.
Trafford Park 11/1041.
Gorton 26/12/41.
Wrexham 8/7/42.

RENUMBERED:
5357 14/2/25.
7435 11/8/46.
67435 21/5/49.

CONDEMNED: 15/12/52.
Into Gor. for cut up 20/12/52.

5359

Gorton.

To traffic 4/1905.

REPAIRS:
Gor. 28/10—16/12/11.**G**.
Gor. 15/10/21—7/1/22.**G**.
Gor. 2/2—12/4/24.**G**.
Gor. 10/7—2/10/26.**G**.
Gor. 15/12/28—2/2/29.**G**.
Gor. 17/10—7/11/31.**G**.
Superheated boiler fitted.
Altered to 13ft gauge.
Gor. 2—23/9/33.**G**.
Double end control
push-pull gear fitted.
WPU gear removed.
Gor. 18/4—9/5/36.**G**.
Fountain lub. to axles.
Gor. 13/11—4/12/37.**G**.
Vacuum P&P gear fitted.
Gor. 15/7—5/8/39.**G**.
Gor. 2—23/3/40.**L**.
Gor. 12—30/8/41.**G**.
Gor. 3—18/12/43.**G**.
Gor. 22/2—15/3/47.**G**.
Gor. 22/1—19/2/49.**G**.
Gor. 20/1—10/2/51.**G**.
Gor. 13—27/10/51.**C/L**.
Gor. 20/6—4/7/53.**G**.

BOILERS:
1020.
479 (new) 16/12/11.
521 (new) 12/4/24.
967 (sup.ex5190) 7/11/31.
733 (ex5190) 23/9/33.
4504 (ex6057) 9/5/36.
298 (ex5199) 4/12/37.
359 (ex5055) 5/8/39.
663 (ex5002) 30/8/41.

975 (exD6 5853) 18/12/43.
348 (ex7438) 15/3/47.
739 (ex7408) 19/2/49.
22908 (ex67419) 10/2/51.
22934 (ex67421) 4/7/53.

SHEDS:
Wrexham 8/11/19.
Trafford Park 23/4/30.
Wrexham 20/1/34.
Chester 30/7/42.

RENUMBERED:
5359 12/4/24.
7436 14/7/46.
67436 19/2/49.

CONDEMNED: 20/2/56.
Into Gor. for cut up 25/2/56.

5114

Gorton.

To traffic 5/1905.

REPAIRS:
Gor. 7/10—11/11/11.**G**.
Gor. 27/3—24/4/15.**G**.
Gor. 4/12/20—15/1/21.**G**.
Gor. 23/6—15/12/23.**G**.
Gor. 1/5—31/7/26.**G**.
Gor. 1/9—20/10/28.**G**.
Gor. 15/8—19/9/31.**G**.
Superheated boiler fitted.
Altered to 13ft gauge.
Gor. 2—23/12/33.**G**.
WPU gear removed.
Gor. 23/11—14/12/35.**G**.
Fountain lub. to axles.
Gor. 22/1—5/2/38.**G**.
Gor. 2—30/3/40.**G**.
Gor. 1—8/2/41.**L**.
Gor. 14—31/10/42.**G**.
Gor. 29/7—22/8/44.**G**.
Gor. 31/8—28/9/46.**G**.
Gor. 6/3—10/4/48.**G**.
Gor. 11—25/12/48.**L**.
Tank leaking.
Gor. 25/2/50.**C/L**.
Tank leaking.
Gor. 22/4—6/5/50.**G**.
Gor. 11—25/11/50.**C/L**.
Tank to weld.
Gor. 8—29/3/52.**G**.
Gor. 3/7—14/8/54.**G**.
Gor. 25/12/54—22/1/55.**C/L**.
Tank repaired.
Gor. 29/12/56—19/1/57.**C/L**.
Tank repaired.

BOILERS:
1022.
1023 (ex115) 11/11/11.

At least until 1939, Gorton continued to put lining on both the front and rear buffer beams.

From June 1942 only NE was used on the tanks but in 12in. instead of the previous 7½in. From March 1938 the classification was put on the buffer beam in 2in. white lettering. Note the wheel still surviving on the door of the smokebox, although it was removed at the April 1947 shopping.

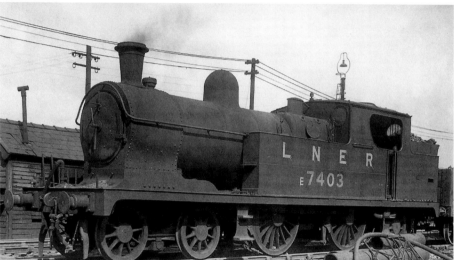

(above) From January 1946 LNER was restored, normally in 7½in. lettering. Note the anti-vacuum valve still on the end of the header after its 3rd May 1947 repair.

(left) From a general repair No.7403 was ex works on 14th December 1946 with LNER in 12in. lettering, which had also been used during 1946 on 6059 (9th March), 7420 (23rd March), 7424 (11th May), 6055 (29th June), 5179 (10th August), 7438 (18th August) and 7437 (28th September). The British Railways E prefix was put on 7403 at a light repair on 24th January 1948 and also on 7410 similarly on 31st January. Manchester (London Road).

356 *(ex171)* 24/4/15.
195 *(new)* 15/12/23.
353 *(sup.new)* 19/9/31.
744 *(exC14 6128)* 23/12/33.
699 *(ex5454)* 14/12/35.
740 *(ex6057)* 5/2/38.
330 *(ex6057)* 30/3/40.
971 *(exD6 5855)* 31/10/42.
742 *(ex5457)* 22/8/44.
740 *(ex7419)* 28/9/46.
661 *(ex7400)* 10/4/48.
365 *(ex67433)* 6/5/50.
365 reno. 22905 25/11/50.
22942 *(new)* 29/3/52.
22964 *(new)* 14/8/54.

SHEDS:
Trafford Park 17/8/18.
Chester 2/6/30.
Northwich 21/9/34.
Trafford Park 26/12/35.
Chester 24/9/36.
Gorton 11/9/39.
Bradford 20/9/41.
Gorton 14/1/42.
Trafford Park 4/4/43.
Chester 29/8/43.
Gorton 21/7/44.
Trafford Park 28/10/45.
Gorton 6/1/46.
Langwith Jct. 24/10/54.
Ardsley 15/5/55.
Gorton 8/1/56.

RENUMBERED:
114c 5/1/24.
5114 31/7/26.
7437 28/9/46.
67437 10/4/48.

CONDEMNED: 5/8/57.
Into Gor. for cut up 10/8/57.

5115

Gorton.

To traffic 7/1905.

REPAIRS:
Gor. 29/7—26/8/11.**G.**
Gor. 21/10/22—7/4/23.**G.**
Gor. 29/8—7/11/25.**G.**
Gor. 12/11/27—7/1/28.**G.**
Gor. 8/3—12/4/30.**G.**
Superheated boiler fitted.
Altered to 13ft gauge.
Gor. 9—30/7/32.**G.**
Gor. 15/12/34—5/1/35.**G.**
Fountain lub. to axles.
Gor. 28/11—12/12/36.**G.**
Gor. 19/11—3/12/38.**G.**
Gor. 30/6—19/7/41.**G.**
Vacuum P&P gear fitted.
Gor. 19/12/42—9/1/43.**G.**
Gor. 18/11—16/12/44.**G.**
Record incomplete.
Gor. 10/4—8/5/48.**G.**
Gor. 4—25/2/50.**G.**
Gor. 8/4/50.**C/L.**
New type push-pull gear.
Gor. 24/5—14/6/52.**G.**
Gor. 11/9—16/10/54.**G.**
Gor. 4—25/2/56.**C/L.**

BOILERS:
1023.
355 *(ex1066)* 26/8/11.
1022 *(ex5453)* 7/4/23.
285 *(sup.new)* 12/4/30.
729 *(ex5310)* 30/7/32.
4501 *(new)* 5/1/35.
746 *(exD6 5852)* 12/12/36.
978 *(ex5456)* 3/12/38.
329 *(ex6058)* 19/7/41.
330 *(ex5114)* 9/1/43.
348 *(ex5009)* 16/12/44.

288 *(ex5179)* ?/8/46.
740 *(ex7437)* 8/5/48.
368 *(ex67431)* 25/2/50.
22946 *(ex67412)* 14/6/52.
22902 *(ex67416)* 16/10/54.

SHEDS:
Wrexham 16/11/18.
Trafford Park 26/2/30.
Gorton 2/1/35.
Neasden 6/8/41.
Gorton 12/2/50.
Copley Hill 17/10/54.
Ardsley 10/3/57.

RENUMBERED:
5115 7/11/25.
7438 18/8/46.
67438 8/5/48.

CONDEMNED: 13/1/58.
Into Gor. for cut up 15/11/58.

5453

Gorton.

To traffic 8/1905.

REPAIRS:
Gor. 15/11/13—28/3/14.**G.**
Gor. 29/4—26/8/22.**G.**
Gor. 10—31/3/23.**G.**
New cylinders & valves.
Gor. 19/9—21/11/25.**G.**
Gor. 16/6—21/7/28.**G.**
Gor. 2/11—7/12/29.**G.**
Gor. 7/5—4/6/32.**G.**
Gor. 30/3—13/4/35.**G.**
Superheated boiler fitted.WPU
gear off.Fountain lub. to axles.
Gor. 8—29/5/37.**G.**
Altered to 13ft gauge.

Gor. 11/11—9/12/39.**G.**
Gor. 3—17/5/41.**L.**
Gor. 22/12/42—23/1/43.**G.**
Gor. 21/7—25/8/45.**G.**
Gor. 23/8—20/9/47.**G.**
Gor. 14/5—4/6/49.**C/L.**
Gor. 20/5—10/6/50.**G.**
Gor. 5/7—9/8/52.**G.**
Gor. 16/4—21/5/55.**G.**
Gor. 3—17/3/56.**C/L.**

BOILERS:
1024.
1022 *(ex1059)* 28/3/14.
536 *(ex spare)* 26/8/22.
900 *(sup.ex5027)* 13/4/35.
4502 *(ex5050)* 29/5/37.
4503 *(ex5455)* 23/1/43.
972 *(ex5050)* 25/8/45.
743 *(ex7435)* 20/9/47.
4528 *(new)* 10/6/50.
22921 *(exC14 67442)* 9/8/52.
22920 *(ex67429)* 21/5/55.

SHEDS:
Wrexham 20/1/22.
Trafford Park 27/4/23.
Chester 20/11/28.
Trafford Park 29/12/29.
Gorton 2/4/37.
Bradford 20/9/41.
Gorton 3/1/42.
Northwich 3/3/46.
Gorton 11/8/46.
Darnall 19/4/53.

RENUMBERED:
5453 21/11/25.
7439 28/4/46.
67439 4/6/49.

CONDEMNED: 14/11/58.
Into Gor. for cut up 15/11/58.

(opposite, bottom) **In January and February 1948 Gorton also applied the E prefix to five which they painted, still unlined black but with BRITISH RAILWAYS, and still with the number on the tank, in unshaded Gill sans but with the modified 6. These were 7432 (24th Jan.), 7414 & 7422 (7th Feb.), 7416 (21st Feb.) and 7400 (28th Feb.).**

On the next ten there was a change, the E being discarded for a figure 6, and the number being moved from the tank to the bunker, but at the front it was still on the buffer beam. 8in. lettering and 12in. numbers were still used. Those in this style, all during 1948, were: 67413 (20th March), 67430 (27th March), 67437 (10th April), 67401 (24th April), 67417 and 67433 (1st May), 67425 and 67438 (8th May), 67407 (15th May) and 67411 (22nd May).

Beginning with No.67431 on 19th June 1948, the number on the front buffer beam was superseded by the fitting of a cast plate on the smokebox door. No.67437 got its plate on 24th December 1948 at a light repair, and until after 21st May 1949 Gorton was still casting the modified 6 and 9 on the plates. Gorton shed.

(left) Whilst still using BRITISH RAILWAYS Gorton changed to 10in. lettering and numbers and with the correct Gill sans 6 and 9 as shown by 67427 ex works on 6th August 1949 but on unlined black.

(below) But when 67420 was ex works on 21st May 1949 with 10in. correct Gill sans characters, it had been given red, cream and grey lining, although its numberplate had the modified 6.

(above) **Having put lining on to 67420, Gorton continued it when the lettering was changed to the British Railways emblem ex works on 30th June 1951. More are known to have had the lining put on, 67412 (3rd May 1952) and 67419 (28th October 1950) but the majority still wore black without lining to their withdrawal. 67439 (10th June 1950) was also lined as was 67418 (3rd March 1951). 67419 is doubtful because on 23rd April 1951 it was unlined.**

(right) **No.67420 lost its lining at its next repair, as it was plain black when ex works on 9th October 1954.**

After the introduction of the British Railways crest in April 1957, only two, 67417 (8th June 1957) and 67418 (21st December 1957) had general repairs and might have been expected to acquire it. But on classes nearing their end, Gorton continued to use up stock of the smaller size of emblem so no C13 got the BR crest. Gorton shed.

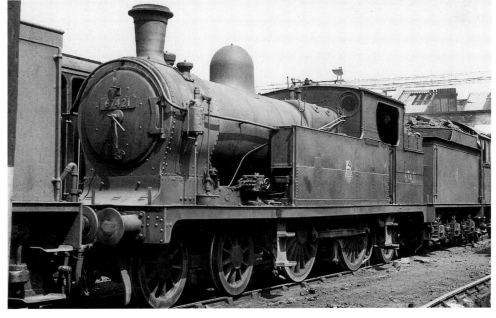

Eleven of the C14 class at the Grouping were unsuperheated and still had the short smokebox. Nottingham (Victoria).

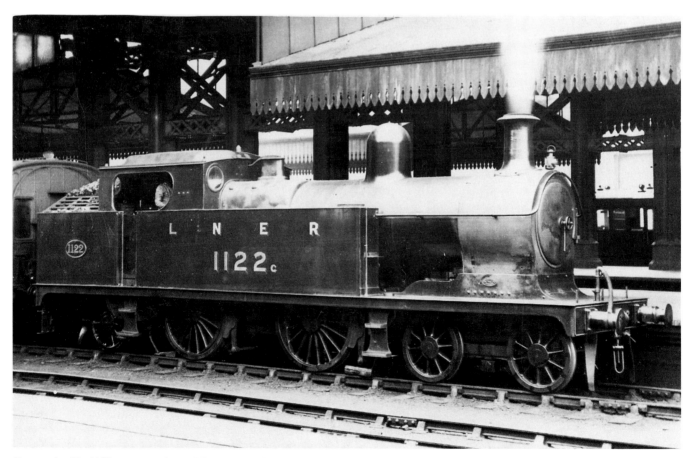

One engine No.1122 was superheated from June 1914 until it went to works on 7th July 1923. The superheater was then taken out but the longer smokebox was retained when ex works on 24th November 1923. The front end of the frame was built to suit the smokebox extension. Nottingham (Victoria).

CLASS C 14

6120

Beyer, Peacock 4926.

To traffic 5/1907.

REPAIRS:
Gor. 1/2—24/5/13.**G.**
Gor. 20/5—24/6/16.**G.**
Gor. 8/7—23/12/22.**G.**
Single chimney fitted.
Gor. 8/11/24—10/1/25.**G.**
Gor. 19/3—14/5/27.**G.**
Gor. 27/4—15/6/29.**G.**
Superheated boiler fitted.
Altered to 13ft gauge.
Gor. 6/6—11/7/31.**G.**
Gor. 3—17/2/34.**G.**
Gor. 16—30/7/38.**G.**
Gor. 11—23/5/42.**G.**
Gor. 12/8—2/9/44.**G.**
Gor. 14—28/9/46.**G.**
Gor. 29/10—19/11/49.**G.**
Gor. 20/9—11/10/52.**G.**
Gor. 21/5—25/6/55.**G.**

BOILERS:
1250.
1254 *(ex1129)* 24/5/13.
1005 *(exC13 2)* 24/6/16.
971 *(sup.new)* 15/6/29.
660 *(ex6123)* 11/7/31.
976 *(exD6 5869)* 17/2/34.
4508 *(ex6121)* 30/7/38.
4511 *(exC13 6065)* 23/5/42.
285 *(exC13 6065)* 2/9/44.
350 *(exC13 67400)* 19/11/49.
22952 *(ex67441)* 11/10/52.
22951 *(ex67441)* 25/6/55.

SHEDS:
Langwith Jct. 3/2/22.
Hitchin 7/5/25.
Annesley 12/12/25.
Ipswich 1/11/34.
King's Lynn 7/3/40.
Ipswich 20/4/40.
Lowestoft 10/4/41.
Norwich 17/8/41.
Neasden 7/11/41.
Gorton 24/1/42.
Trafford Park 25/1/42.
Ardsley 3/4/43.
Copley Hill 4/3/51.
Ardsley 24/6/51.
Gorton 19/4/53.

RENUMBERED:
6120 10/1/25.
7440 7/7/46.
67440 19/11/49.

CONDEMNED: 4/7/57.
Into Gor. for cut up 6/7/57.

6121

Beyer, Peacock 4927.

To traffic 5/1907.

REPAIRS:
Gor. 19/3—21/5/21.**G.**
Gor. 5/5—25/8/23.**G.**
Gor. 6/2—30/6/26.**G.**
Superheated boiler fitted.
Gor. 12/1—16/2/29.**G.**
Gor. 17/1—14/2/31.**G.**
Gor. 3—17/6/33.**G.**
Altered to 13ft gauge.
Gor. 6—27/7/35.**G.**
Gor. 11—25/6/38.**G.**
Gor. 18—25/3/39.**L.**
Gor. 23/11—7/12/40.**G.**
Gor. 7—31/10/42.**H.**
Gor. 10/6—1/7/44.**G.**
Gor. 12—26/10/46.**G.**
Gor. 2—16/4/49.**G.**
Gor. 5—19/8/50.**C/L.**
After collision.
Gor. 2—30/8/52.**G.**
Gor. 5/3—9/4/55.**G.**
Gor. 21/4—12/5/56.**C/L.**
After collision.

BOILERS:
1251.
689 *(sup.new)* 30/6/26.
298 *(ex6129)* 17/6/33.
4508 *(new)* 27/7/35.
349 *(exC13 5028)* 25/6/38.
691 *(ex6124)* 7/12/40.
368 *(exC13 5028)* 1/7/44.
521 *(exC13 7426)* 26/10/46.
362 *(exC13 7426)* 16/4/49.
22951 *(exC13 67439)* 30/8/52.
22946 *(exC13 67438)* 9/4/55.

SHEDS:
Langwith Jct. 3/2/22.
Annesley ?/12/27.
Gorton 9/2/37.
Northwich 15/2/37.

Colwick 21/2/40.
Trafford Park 7/1/42.
Neasden 17/1/43.
Ardsley 15/2/43.
Gorton 24/6/51.

RENUMBERED:
1121c 25/8/23.
6121 30/6/26.
7441 7/7/46.
67441 16/4/49.

CONDEMNED: 5/8/57.
Into Gor. for cut up 10/8/57.

6122

Beyer, Peacock 4928.

To traffic 5/1907.

REPAIRS:
Gor. 24/1—13/6/14.**G.**
Superheated boiler fitted.
Gor. 20/3—22/5/20.**G.**
Gor. 7/7—24/11/23.**G.**
Saturated boiler fitted.
Gor. 3/10—26/12/25.**G.**
Gor. 17/12/27—11/2/28.**G.**
Gor. 2/11—14/12/29.**G.**
Gor. 20/2—12/3/32.**G.**
Superheated boiler fitted.
Gor. 26/5—9/6/34.**G.**
Altered to 13ft gauge.
WPU gear removed.
Gor. 6—27/6/36.**G.**
Gor. 19/8—23/9/39.**G.**
Gor. 28/4—15/5/43.**G.**
Gor. 16/2—9/3/46.**G.**
Gor. 26/2—19/3/49.**G.**
Gor. 10/6—29/7/50.**G.**
Gor. 12—19/5/51.**C/L.**
Gor. 7—28/6/52.**G.**
Gor. 21—28/2/53.**C/L.**
Gor. 12/2—12/3/55.**C/L.**
Gor. 4/6—9/7/55.**G.**

BOILERS:
1252
1009 *(sup.exC13 27)* 13/6/14.
134 *(sat. new)* 24/11/23.
904 *(exC13 5179)* 12/3/32.
686 *(exD6 5875)* 9/6/34.
368 *(ex6131)* 27/6/36.
298 *(exC13 5359)* 23/9/39.
757 *(ex6125)* 15/5/43.

161 *(ex6125)* 9/3/46.
4520 *(new)* 19/3/49.
4531 *(new)* 29/7/50.
4531 reno. 22921 19/5/51.
22947 *(ex67444)* 28/6/52.
22921 *(exC13 67439)* 9/7/55.

SHEDS:
Annesley 5/18.
Colwick 2/4/28.
Ipswich 26/6/35.
Lowestoft 7/3/40.
Norwich 17/8/41.
Neasden 7/11/41.
Gorton 31/12/41.
Trafford Park 7/5/42.
Ardsley 19/7/43.
Lincoln 28/3/48.
Wrexham 11/7/48.

RENUMBERED:
1122c 24/11/23.
6122 26/12/25.
7442 7/7/46.
67442 19/3/49.

CONDEMNED: 29/11/57.
Into Gor. for cut up 30/11/57.

6123

Beyer, Peacock 4929.

To traffic 5/1907.

REPAIRS:
Gor. 14/3—16/5/14.**G.**
Gor. 2/7/21—21/1/22.**G.**
Tux. 24/10—29/12/23.**G.**
Gor. 15/8/25—16/1/26.**G.**
Superheated boiler fitted.
Altered to 13ft gauge.
Gor. 11/2—31/3/28.**G.**
Gor. 28/3—25/4/31.**G.**
Gor. 6—20/5/33.**G.**
Gor. 2—16/3/35.**G.**
Over 13ft gauge.
Gor. 29/5—19/6/37.**G.**
Altered to 13ft gauge.
Gor. 29/10—26/11/38.**L.**
Gor. 24/8—12/9/42.**G.**
Gor. 5/5—9/6/45.**G.**
Gor. 27/3—24/4/48.**G.**
Gor. 5/5—2/6/51.**G.**
Gor. 10/4—15/5/54.**G.**
Gor. 21/1—4/2/56.**C/L.**

WORKS CODES:- Cw - Cowlairs. Dar- Darlington. Don - Doncaster. Ghd - Gateshead. Gor - Gorton. Inv - Inverurie. Nor - Norwich. Str - Stratford.
REPAIR CODES:- **C/H** - Casual Heavy. **C/L** - Casual Light. **G** - General. **H**- Heavy. **H/I** - Heavy Intermediate. **L** - Light. **L/I** - Light Intermediate. **N/C** - Non-Classified.

(above) **Between January 1926 (6123) and January 1935 (6125) the whole class was superheated and most of them got an anti-vacuum valve on the end of the header. Note that the cab cut-out has been reduced and not just in makeshift manner but no others were so observed and as No.7445 (*see* page 85, bottom) the cut-out was back to normal.**

(left) **The standard position for the anti-vacuum valve was the top centre of the smokebox, behind the chimney, but the side mounting could still be seen through to December 1959 (*see* page 89, bottom).**

Instead of getting the usual 18-element superheater some got the fifteen element type in boilers which had been on Class D6 engines. These could be identified by the retention of a tall dome.

When superheated by the LNER, either Detroit or Eureka sight feed lubricator in the cab was used for the cylinders and valves. None of the class got mechanical lubricators.

(above) Sanding was by gravity and in early LNER days some had windshields fitted at the pipe ends to help keep the sand on the rail head. No.6120 still had the windshields to March 1927 *(see* page 82, top).

(right) By 1946 steam applied sanding was being fitted and this type then became standard for the C14's.

6123 cont./
After collision.
Gor. 27/10—3/11/56.**C/L.**
Gor. 22/6/57. *Not repaired.*

BOILERS:
 1253.
 1024 *(exC13 453)* 16/5/14.
 678A *(ex1127)* 21/1/22.
 660 *(sup.new)* 16/1/26.
 330 *(new)* 25/4/31.
 731 *(ex6126)* 20/5/33.
 110 *(exD6 5852)* 16/3/35.
 161 *(exD6 5859)* 19/6/37.
 361 *(ex6126)* 12/9/42.
 327 *(ex6130)* 9/6/45.
 279 *(exD6 2106)* 24/4/48.
22923 *(new)* 2/6/51.
22931 *(exC13 67425)* 15/5/54.

SHEDS:
Annesley 16/5/19.
Langwith Jct. *by* 24/10/23.
Ipswich 26/6/35.
King's Lynn 7/3/40.
Ipswich 20/4/40.
Cambridge 26/5/40.
Lowestoft 12/12/40.
Norwich 17/8/41.
Ardsley 29/10/41.
Gorton 15/5/55.

RENUMBERED:
 1123c 29/12/23.
 6123 16/1/26.
 7443 21/7/46.
67443 24/4/48.

CONDEMNED: 24/6/57.
Cut up at Gorton.

6124

Beyer, Peacock 4930.

To traffic 5/1907.

REPAIRS:
Gor. 7/10—4/11/11.**G.**
Gor. 15/3—24/5/13.**G.**
Tux. 11/6—15/9/20.**H.**
Gor. 17/3—27/10/23.**G.**
Gor. 10/10—19/12/25.**G.**
Gor. 18/2—7/4/28.**G.**
Superheated boiler fitted.
Altered to 13ft gauge.
Gor. 6/12/30—10/1/31.**G.**
Gor. 24/6—15/7/33.**G.**
Gor. 15/8—26/9/36.**G.**
Gor. 30/7—13/8/38.**G.**
Gor. 13—27/7/40.**G.**
Gor. 2—31/10/42.**H.**
Gor. 15—25/9/43.**G.**

Gor. 23/3—13/4/46.**G.**
Gor. 10—24/9/49.**G.**
Gor. 3—24/5/52.**G.**
Gor. 29/1—26/2/55.**G.**

BOILERS:
 1254.
 1257 *(ex1127)* 4/11/11.
 1011 *(exC13 29)* 24/5/13.
 115 *(new)* 27/10/23.
 738 *(sup.new)* 7/4/28.
 206 *(exC13 6064)* 15/7/33.
 686 *(ex6122)* 26/9/36.
 691 *(exC13 6059)* 13/8/38.
 660 *(exC13 5018)* 27/7/40.
 741 *(exC13 6059)* 13/4/46.
 688 *(exC13 67413)* 24/9/49.
22945 *(exC13 67433)* 24/5/52.
22905 *(exC13 67412)* 26/2/55.

SHEDS:
Annesley 26/5/19.
Colwick 2/4/28.
Annesley 26/1/29.
Langwith Jct. 16/5/39.
Colwick 24/11/40.
Trafford Park 7/1/42.
Ardsley 5/6/42.
Gorton 22/3/53.

RENUMBERED:
 1124c 27/10/23.
 6124 19/12/25.
 7444 13/4/46.
67444 24/9/49.

CONDEMNED: 3/7/57.
Into Gor. for cut up 6/7/57.

6125

Beyer, Peacock 4931.

To traffic 5/1907.

REPAIRS:
Gor. 18/12/15—19/2/16.**G.**
Gor. 8/4—22/7/22.**G.**
Gor. 27/9/24—9/5/25.**G.**
Gor. 28/5—16/7/27.**G.**
Gor. 4—25/1/30.**G.**
Gor. 11/6—2/7/32.**G.**
Gor. 22/12/34—19/1/35.**G.**
Superheated boiler fitted.
Altered to 13ft gauge.
WPU gear removed.
Gor. 10—31/7/37.**G.**
Gor. 8—22/6/40.**G.**
Gor. 4—27/3/43.**G.**
Gor. 17/11—8/12/45.**G.**
Gor. 11/9—2/10/48.**G.**
Gor. 1—22/9/51.**G.**
Gor. 19/6—31/7/54.**G.**

Gor. 2—30/3/57.**G.**
Gor. 19/12/59. *Not repaired.*

BOILERS:
 1255.
 1015 *(exC13 457)* 19/2/16.
 479 *(exC13 359)* 9/5/25.
 1260 *(exC13 6060)* 25/1/30.
 134 *(ex6122)* 2/7/32.
 729 *(exC13 5115)* 19/1/35.
 757 *(ex6129)* 22/6/40.
 161 *(ex6123)* 27/3/43.
 359 *(exC13 5020)* 8/12/45.
 332 *(exC13 7410)* 2/10/48.
22932 *(exC13 67414)* 22/9/51.
22918 *(exC13 67409)* 31/7/54.
22950 *(ex spare)* 30/3/57.

SHEDS:
Neasden 11/11/21.
Langwith Jct. 15/5/25.
Colwick 20/9/30.
Langwith Jct. 11/2/31.
Colwick 8/1/32.
Langwith Jct. 23/9/33.
Ipswich 28/6/35.
London Passenger Transport
Board at Neasden 24/1/38.
Ipswich 23/3/38.
Gorton 28/12/42.
Ardsley 27/3/43.
Gorton 28/12/52.
Barnsley. 7/7/57.

RENUMBERED:
 6125 9/5/25.
 7445 21/7/46.
67445 2/10/48.

CONDEMNED: 22/12/59.
Cut up at Gorton.

6126

Beyer, Peacock 4932.

To traffic 5/1907.

REPAIRS:
Gor. 4/3—25/5/12.**G.**
Gor. 4/10—20/12/13.**G.**
Gor. 27/12/19—13/3/20.**G.**
Gor. 14/10/22—20/1/23.**G.**
Tux. 26/3—10/7/25.**H.**
Gor. 24/9—26/11/27.**G.**
Superheated boiler fitted.
Gor. 19/10—15/11/30.**G.**
Altered to 13ft gauge.
Gor. 11—25/3/33.**G.**
Over 13ft gauge.
Gor. 4—18/5/35.**G.**
Altered to 13ft gauge.
Gor. 25/12/37—22/1/38.**G.**

Gor. 20/6—11/7/42.**G.**
Gor. 16/12/44—6/1/45.**G.**
Gor. 3/7—14/8/48.**G.**
Gor. 18/8—15/9/51.**G.**
Gor. 3/7—14/8/54.**G.**

BOILERS:
 1256.
 1260 *(ex1130)* 25/5/12.
 1257 *(ex1124)* 20/12/13.
 1287 *(ex spare)* 13/3/20.
 731 *(sup.new)* 26/11/27.
 1794 *(exC13 5018)* 25/3/33.
 4505 *(new)* 18/5/35.
 361 *(exC13 5454)* 22/1/38.
 4508 *(ex6120)* 11/7/42.
 369 *(exD6 5871)* 6/1/45.
 330 *(exC13 7428)* 14/8/48.
22930 *(exC13 67430)* 15/9/51.
22963 *(new)* 14/8/54.

SHEDS:
Woodford 17/3/22.
Langwith Jct *after* 1/1/23.
Hitchin 31/12/27.
Hatfield 4/3/30.
Colwick 27/11/30.
Annesley 11/12/30.
Ipswich 28/6/35.
London Passenger Transport
Board at Neasden 22/1/38.
Ipswich 9/3/38.
Woodford 4/5/38.
Ipswich 11/10/38.
King's Lynn 7/3/40.
Ipswich 16/5/40.
Cambridge 26/5/40.
Lowestoft 12/12/40.
Norwich 17/8/41.
Ardsley 30/10/41.
Gorton 15/5/55.

RENUMBERED:
 6126 10/7/25.
 7446 21/7/46.
67446 14/8/48.

CONDEMNED: 27/5/57.
Into Gor. for cut up 1/6/57.

6127

Beyer, Peacock 4933.

To traffic 6/1907.

REPAIRS:
Gor. 19/8—23/9/11.**G.**
Gor. 14/5—18/6/21.**G.**
Tux. 28/12/23—7/3/24.**H.**
Gor. 21/5—23/7/27.**G.**
Gor. 26/7—30/8/30.**G.**
Superheated boiler fitted.

Tank equalising pipes were originally of large rectangular section and there were four inward sloping coal rails on the bunker top, matching the profile of the bunker back plate, and these rails were open.

There were changes to both these details in the 1930's. Smaller and circular equalising pipes were put on and four vertical rails, with plating behind, were fitted to sides and back of the bunker. Note that the top lamp iron has been moved on to the smokebox door.

(above) Four, Nos.7441, 7444, 7450 and 7451, did not get the vertical bunker rails. On these engines the inward sloping rails were reduced from four to three with the top one changed from flat to angle iron. Ipswich.

(left) No.67445 in September 1953 with bunker rails altered and using a boiler fitted in September 1951 with which the anti-vacuum valve was the standard type behind the chimney (*but see* page 89, bottom). Manchester (London Road).

At Grouping all except one still had the Robinson tapered chimney, and Ramsbottom type safety valves with the cast iron enclosure.

6127 cont./
Altered to 13ft gauge.
Gor. 15/10—5/11/32.**G.**
WPU gear removed.
Gor. 20/10—10/11/34.**G.**
Gor. 23/1—13/2/37.**G.**
Gor. 4—25/5/40.**G.**
Gor. 1—11/9/43.**G.**
Gor. 1—22/9/45.**H.**
Gor. 4—11/10/47.**L.**
After collision.
Gor. 14—28/8/48.**G.**
Gor. 14/5—11/6/49.**L.**
Gor. 13—27/1/51.**G.**
Gor. 7—28/3/53.**G.**
Gor. 15/1—12/2/55.**C/L.**
Gor. 14/1—18/2/56.**G.**

BOILERS:
  1257.
    678A *(new)* 23/9/11.
    1259 *(exC13 199)* 18/6/21.
    743 *(sup.exD6 5873)* 30/8/30.
    279 *(exC13 5027)* 5/11/32.
    662 *(exC13 5171)* 10/11/34.
    369 *(exC13 6063)* 13/2/37.
    731 *(exD6 5876)* 25/5/40.
    694 *(exD6 5869)* 11/9/43.
    4508 *(ex6126)* 22/9/45.
    288 *(exC13 7438)* 28/8/48.
  22907 *(ex7448)* 27/1/51.
  22926 *(exC13 67420)* 28/3/53.
  22933 *(ex67450)* 18/2/56 .

SHEDS:
Annesley 23/9/21.
Langwith Jct. *by* 28/12/23.
Ipswich 26/6/35.
Bradford 14/5/50.
Gorton 24/6/51.
Barnsley 3/11/57.

RENUMBERED:
  6127 7/3/24.
  7447 21/7/46.
  67447 28/8/48.

CONDEMNED: 2/12/58.
Into Gor. for cut up 6/12/58.

_____

6128

Beyer, Peacock 4934.

To traffic 6/1907.

REPAIRS:
Gor. 19/8—21/10/22.**G.**
Gor. 5/4—19/7/24.**G.**
Gor. 28/5—23/7/27.**G.**
Gor. 12/5—7/7/28.**G.**
Superheated boiler fitted.
Altered to 13ft gauge.

Gor. 14/3—11/4/31.**G.**
Gor. 22/7—5/8/33.**G.**
Over 13ft gauge.
Gor. 1—22/6/35.**G.**
Gor. 27/3—17/4/37.**G.**
Altered to 13ft gauge.
Gor. 20/7—10/8/40.**G.**
Gor. 26/5—19/6/43.**G.**
Gor. 16—30/12/44.**G.**
Gor. 11/10—1/11/47.**G.**
Gor. 29/7—12/8/50.**G.**
Gor. 1—15/12/51.**C/L.**
Gor. 23/5—20/6/53.**G.**
Gor. 9/6—7/7/56.**G.**

BOILERS:
  1258.
    753 *(new)* 19/7/24.
    744 *(sup.new)* 7/7/28.
    909 *(exD6 5872)* 5/8/33.
  1794 *(ex6126)* 22/6/35.
  4509 *(exC13 5009)* 17/4/37.
    688 *(exC13 6056)* 10/8/40.
    298 *(ex6122)* 19/6/43.
    690 *(ex spare)* 30/12/44.
  4516 *(new)* 1/11/47.
  4518 *(exC13 7422)* 12/8/50.
  4518 reno. 22937 15/12/51.
  22927 *(exC13 67411)* 20/6/53.
  22943 *(ex spare)* 7/7/56.

SHEDS:
Annesley 6/18.
Langwith Jct *after* 1/1/23.
Colwick 23/9/33.
Ipswich 26/6/35.
Bradford 14/5/50.
Gorton 24/6/51.
Barnsley 7/7/57.

RENUMBERED:
  6128 19/7/24.
  7448 21/7/46.
  67448 12/8/50.

CONDEMNED: 18/6/59.
Into Gor. for cut up 20/6/59.

_____

6129

Beyer, Peacock 4935.

To traffic 6/1907.

REPAIRS:
Gor. 11/11—9/12/11.**G.**
Gor. 5/4—3/5/13.**G.**
Gor. 5/6—18/9/15.**G.**
Gor. 28/10—31/3/23.**G.**
Gor. 2/5—25/7/25.**G.**
Gor. 23/4—9/7/27.**G.**
Gor. 17/5—21/6/30.**G.**
Superheated boiler fitted.

Altered to 13ft gauge.
Gor. 11/3—1/4/33.**G.**
Gor. 19/1—2/2/35.**G.**
Gor. 21/11—5/12/36.**G.**
Gor. 20/1—10/2/40.**G.**
Gor. 21/5—5/6/43.**G.**
Gor. 26—27/11/43.**L.**
Gor. 29/6—10/8/46.**G.**
Gor. 14/5—4/6/49.**G.**
Gor. 19/5—16/6/51.**G.**
Gor. 19/1—1/3/52.**C/L.**
After collision.
Gor. 29/8—19/9/53.**G.**

BOILERS:
  1259.
  1254 *(ex1124)* 9/12/11.
  1250 *(ex1120)* 3/5/13.
  1007 *(exC13 18)* 18/9/15.
    298 *(sup.new)* 21/6/30.
    327 *(exD6 5879)* 1/4/33.
    757 *(exC13 5455)* 5/12/36.
    744 *(exC13 5171)* 10/2/40.
    279 *(exC13 6060)* 5/6/43.
    978 *(exD6 5871)* 10/8/46.
    361 *(exC13 7435)* 4/6/49.
  22924 *(exC13 67418)* 16/6/51.
  22937 *(ex 67448)* 19/9/53.

SHEDS:
Annesley 6/18.
Langwith Jct. 16/1/28.
Colwick 5/10/31.
Woodford 25/8/33.
Colwick 2/11/33.
Ipswich 26/6/35.
London Passenger Transport
Board at Neasden 24/1/38
Ipswich 29/3/38.
Lowestoft 30/12/40.
Norwich 17/8/41.
Ardsley 25/10/41.
Lincoln 21/3/48.
Wrexham 11/7/48.

RENUMBERED:
  6129 25/7/25.
  7449 10/8/46.
  67449 4/6/49.

CONDEMNED: 2/12/57.
Into Gor. for cut up 7/12/57.

_____

6130

Beyer, Peacock 4936.

To traffic 6/1907.

REPAIRS:
Gor. 28/11/11—17/2/12.**G.**
Gor. 10/4—15/5/15.**G.**
Gor. 19/1—30/3/18.**G.**

Tux. 3/12/20—22/2/21.**H.**
Gor. 10/2—14/4/23.**G.**
Tux. 7/10—31/12/25.**H.**
Gor. 4/2—31/3/28.**G.**
Gor. 22/11/30—24/1/31.**G.**
Superheated boiler fitted.
Altered to 13ft gauge.
Gor. 15—29/7/33.**G.**
Gor. 6—20/7/35.**G.**
Gor. 3—24/7/37.**G.**
Gor. 5—26/4/41.**G.**
Gor. 9/12/44—6/1/45.**G.**
Gor. 7/6—5/7/47.**G.**
Gor. 19—26/3/49.**C/L.**
Gor. 29/7—19/8/50.**G.**
Gor. 20—27/10/51.**C/L.**
Gor. 28/3—2/5/53.**G.**
Gor. 24/9—29/10/55.**G.**
Gor. 9/1/60. *Not repaired.*

BOILERS:
  1260.
  1259 *(ex1129)* 17/2/12.
    345 *(exC13 1056)* 15/5/15.
  1024 *(ex1123)* 14/4/23.
    329 *(sup.new)* 24/1/31.
    689 *(ex6121)* 29/7/33.
  4507 *(new)* 20/7/35.
    353 *(exC13 5357)* 24/7/37.
    327 *(exC13 5027)* 26/4/41.
    349 *(ex spare)* 6/1/45.
  4501 *(exC13 7418)* 5/7/47.
  4520 *(ex 67442)* 19/8/50.
  4520 reno. 22935 27/10/51.
  22933 *(exC13 67400)* 2/5/53.
  22913 *(exC13 67403)* 29/10/55.

SHEDS:
Heaton Mersey 3/2/22.
Langwith Jct. 26/5/23.
Annesley 14/8/35.
Woodford 9/4/38.
Ipswich 11/10/38.
Bradford 14/5/50.
Gorton 24/6/51.

RENUMBERED:
  6130 31/12/25.
  7450 25/7/46.
  67450 26/3/49.

CONDEMNED: 20/1/60.
Cut up at Gorton.

_____

6131

Beyer, Peacock 4937.

To traffic 6/1907.

REPAIRS:
Gor. 21/6—27/9/13.**G.**
Gor. 11/11—23/12/22.**G.**

(above) **The 'odd one out', No.1120, was ex works on 23rd December 1922 and ex paint shop on the 10th February 1923 fitted with an experimental 'single piece' chimney which it kept to March 1927; no others in the class got this type of chimney.**

(left) **All were subsequently fitted with the shorter 'plant pot' type chimney and they also lost the cover around the safety valves.**

No.6125, whilst still saturated and over 13ft 0in. high from the rail. It was not brought within the composite loading gauge until it was superheated in January 1935 when Class Part 1 became extinct.

Beginning with No.7448 on 1st November 1947, new boilers had Ross 'pop' safety valves, but only that one and Nos. 67442, 67443 and 67450 got the Ross 'pop' valves.

Apart from No. 6127 (see page 79, bottom), the upper lamp iron remained on top of the smokebox until during the 1939-1945 war.

During, or soon after the war, most had the wheel for the smokebox door fastening replaced by a handle, but No.7445's wheel survived an 8th December 1945 repair and it was not at works again until 11th September 1948.

After Grouping, Gorton paint shop, on 10th February 1923, turned out Nos.1120 and 1131 still in GCR green but with tank lettered and numbered as shown. No others got the green paint.

6131 cont./
Gor. 28/3—7/11/25.**G.**
Gor. 28/5—23/7/27.**G.**
Gor. 2/6—14/7/28.**G.**
Gor. 1/6—6/7/29.**G.**
Superheated boiler fitted.
Altered to 13ft gauge.
Gor. 16/1—6/2/32.**G.**
Gor. 7—28/4/34.**G.**
Gor. 2—16/5/36.**G.**
Gor. 16/4—7/5/38.**G.**
Gor. 7/12/40—4/1/41.**G.**
Gor. 9—27/11/43.**G.**
Gor. 18/5—10/8/46.**G.**
Gor. 5—26/2/49.**G.**
Gor. 29/12/51—19/1/52.**G.**
Gor. 19/6—31/7/54.**G.**

BOILERS:
  1261.
  1018 *(exC13 456)* 27/9/13.
  678A *(ex1123)* 7/11/25.
  972 *(sup.new)* 6/7/29.
  368 *(new)* 28/4/34.
  755 *(exD6 5871)* 16/5/36.
  4505 *(ex6126)* 7/5/38.
  349 *(ex6121)* 4/1/41.
  744 *(ex6129)* 27/11/43.
  4510 *(exC13 5457)* 10/8/46.
  967 *(exC13 7419)* 26/2/49.
22938 *(exC13 67427)* 19/1/52.
22941 *(exC13 67431)* 31/7/54.

SHEDS:
Heaton Mersey 3/2/22.
Annesley 16/2/23.
Colwick 2/4/28.
Annesley 19/8/35.
Langwith Jct. 15/5/39.
Colwick 28/8/40.
Trafford Park 7/1/42.
Ardsley 3/4/43.
Gorton 24/6/51.

RENUMBERED:
  6131 7/11/25.
  7451 10/8/46.
67451 26/2/49.

CONDEMNED: 21/1/57.
Into Gor. for cut up 26/1/57.

___

(left) **Nos.1126 (31st March), 1129 (19th May) and 1130 (26th May), all in 1923, were in black with single red lining and the only others to have the full points and the ampersand. These dates were ex paint shop. The next four, Nos.1121, 1122, 1123 and 1124, simply had LNER but they also had the area suffix C added to the number (*see page 74, bottom*).**

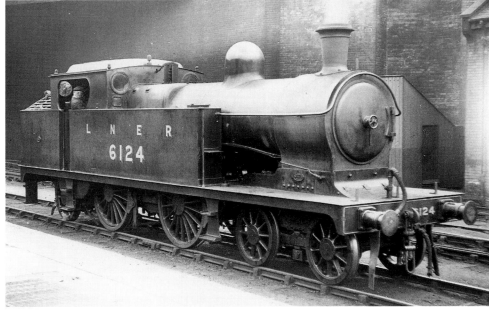

(above) **The other three went straight to LNER and the 1924 number, Nos. 6127 (7th March 1924), 6125 (9th May 1925) and 6128 (19th July 1924). Black paint with single red lining continued to be standard until November 1941.**

(right) **This 1929 photo shows No.6124 as ex works on 7th April 1928 and there seems to be no evidence of red lining. It is possible that Gorton did turn out some in unlined black.**

From June 1942 only NE was put on in 12in. letters and some still had these when renumbered. No. 6127 was ex works on 22nd September 1945 with NE which it kept to 14th August 1948 so that engine did not have LNER restored. It was changed to 7447 at Ipswich shed on Sunday 21st July 1946.

LNER was restored from mid-January 1946 and on tank engines Gorton frequently used 12in. transfers for the purpose. No.6120 became 7440 at Ardsley shed on 7th July 1946 but was ex works as shown on 28th September 1946. No.7441 got this style when ex works on the 26th October 1946, but 7450, ex works on 5th July 1947, had 7$\frac{1}{2}$in. LNER letters (*see* page 77, bottom). No.7444, out on 13th April 1946, had 12in. LNER lettering as did 7449 and 7451 out 10th August 1946.

No.67443 was ex works on 24th April 1948 with 12in. numbers on the bunker and 8in. lettering on the tanks, the front-end number being on the buffer beam. It had Gill sans except for the modified 6 and was the only one in this style.

The next two, 67446 (14th August 1948) and 67447 (28th August 1948) had the bunker numbers reduced to 8in. to match the lettering and they had smokebox number plates fitted. Both had the modified 6 on both bunker and plate, but 67445, ex works on 2nd October 1948, had the correct 6 on the bunker and on the plate.

When 67451 was ex works on 26th February 1949, it not only had 10in. characters in correct Gill sans but also had red, cream and grey lining.

Gorton persisted with lining on others after the change to the British Railways emblem but only Nos.67442 and 67447 were so recorded.

By 1955 all pretension at lining had been discarded and unlined black became the norm.

Indeed, time spent on lining would have been completely wasted, the engines getting so little cleaning that in this May 1957 photo, even the emblem is difficult to discern.

In March 1957 No.67445 was fitted with a boiler built in June 1949 but in which the superheater header still had the anti-vacuum valve at the end and not in the central position. This was the last of the class to be repaired so C14 missed out on getting the second British Railways emblem. Wath.

All three C17's had been built at Melton Constable works, No.41 in December 1904, No.20 in February 1909 and No.9 in March 1910. The LNER retained these numbers but with a cipher in front of them. Between May and November 1937 Stratford put them into unlined black with shaded transfers. 09 in May had normal spacing for LNER and numbers; on 041 (September) and 020 (November) it was wider. All were in the livery shown to their withdrawal.

In their LNER days they were remarkable as a class without any detail differences.

CLASS C 17

041

Melton Constable 10.

To traffic 12/1904.

REPAIRS:
Str. 18/9/37.**G.**

BOILERS:
41.
41 18/9/37.

SHED:
Melton Constable *at* 1/10/36.

RENUMBERED:
041 18/9/37.
Allocated 7503.

CONDEMNED: 14/1/44.
Cut up at Stratford.

020

Melton Constable 11.

To traffic 2/1909.

REPAIRS:
MC. 6/33.**G.**
Str. 7/9—12/11/37.**G.**
Str. 19/7—26/7/41.**L.**
Str. 2/2/42. *Not repaired.*

STORED:
25/11/37 to 29/6/38.
10/10/38 to 31/5/39.

BOILERS:
20.
20 6/33.

SHEDS:
Melton Constable *at* 1/10/36.
Yarmouth Beach 30/6/38.
Melton Constable 28/9/39.
Yarmouth Beach 8/10/39.
Melton Constable 13/12/39.

RENUMBERED:
020 12/11/37

CONDEMNED: 11/4/42.
Cut up at Stratford.

09

Melton Constable 12.

To traffic 3/1910.

REPAIRS:
Str. 5/37.**G.**
Str. 9/43.**L.**

BOILERS:
9.
9 5/37.

SHED:
Melton Constable *at* 1/10/36.

RENUMBERED:
09 *by* 2/37.
Allocated 7504.

CONDEMNED: 21/7/44.
Cut up at Stratford.

As taken over, the 1904 built engine did have a very slight difference from the two. It had a slightly elliptical cast brass numberplate on the bunker, with red backing, the company initials, used from 1930 were pure LMS.

On the other two there were larger cut-out brass numbers fixed directly on to the sides of the bunker, the top of which never carried any coal rails.

For running with either end leading they had the Whittaker tablet exchange apparatus on both sides of the engine. The Deeley type smokebox doors with six dog clips were put on in the late 1920's and the sloping top to the side tanks was a 1933/1934 alteration.

Until 1930 the M&GNR passenger engines were painted willow green with black and white lining. The circular armorial was enclosed in a stylised diamond. Although described as 'green' the colour was between gamboge yellow and light brown.

From 1930 a darker colour described as umber was used and the application of lining was considerably reduced whilst the elaborate shaded lettering disappeared.

There were no shades of opinion as to colour when the LNER took over. It was uncompromisingly plain black and without any lining.